MW00815632

BLOCK
THE
CHESAPEAKE

by
J.H. Robertson

To a fellow History Buff! Jack Robertson

BIM-GUS PUBLISHERS
573 Saddlehorn Drive
Chesapeake, Virginia 23322

BLOCK THE CHESAPEAKE

Copyright (c) 1997
John H. Robertson

All rights reserved. No parts of this book
may be reproduced in any form, except
for brief quotations to be used in a
review or a student's work, without
written permission of the author.

Library of Congress Catalog Card Number: 97-92834
ISBN: 1-57502-676-7

SPECIAL THANKS TO:

My editor, my son, Alan T. Robertson.
Many thanks,   you put the polish on the manuscript.

My friend Frank Smith who labored long to put my
ideas for a cover into the finished product.

The Reference Department of The Virginia Beach
  Public   Library who rounded up those books for me.

Cover photo is of a painting   the author owns.

Published by
BIM-GUS PUBLISHERS
573 Saddlehorn Drive
Chesapeake, Va. 23322

Printed by
Morris Publishing
3212 E. Hwy. 30
Kearney, NE. 68847

For additional copies or information, contact
BIM-GUS PUBLISHERS: 757-482-9632

DEDICATION

One cannot say enough in admiration of those stout-hearted men who had the fortitude and tenacity to stay in the field through all the adversities of the American Revolution----while the "summer soldier and the sunshine patriot" picked up their gear and went home at the first sign of real trouble.

As a conscript in a much later war, I'd like to say, "Here's to you comrades, the first of many who, down through the years, answered our country's call for service---and especially to those who did not make it back home."

AND:

      A special dedication to a great teacher, Annie Bell Crowder, who taught me to love American History---and ; " whatever you write, write it correctly".

PREFACE

I am a history buff---particularly interested in the Revolutionary War period. I think I owe this interest to my sixth grade history teacher, Miss Annie Bell Crowder. Coming from Roxboro, N.C., she knew all about the Halifax Declaration, Cornwallis' march through the Carolinas, and his campaign in Virginia. We first met in 1935, three years after the sesquicentennial celebration of the end of the War at Yorktown.

In 1975 I was appointed to the Virginia Beach Bicentennial Committee. Our commemoration project was to be the Battle Off The Capes of Virginia. As the Vice-chairman, I felt I should learn as much as possible about the battle. Over the next five years, I visited libraries and museums, contacted readers at others, and borrowed micro-film from libraries all over this country, Canada, and Great Britain. My research material eventually filled three file drawers and several book shelves. With all of this, something had to be done---this book is that something.

J.H. ROBERTSON

CONTENTS

ILLUSTRATIONS

ACKNOWLEDGEMENTS

I could not have put this story together without having access to several outstanding collections of papers and manuscripts:

1. The Public Records Office, London, England.
    a. P.R.O. 30-11, The Cornwallis papers.
    b. P.R.O. 30-20. The Rodney Papers.
    c. P.R.O. 30-8.   The Chatham papers.
    d. ADM. 51.-33 Log, *ALCIDE*
    e. ADM. 51-475 Log, *INTREPID*
    f. ADM. 51-732 Log, *PRINCESSA*
    g. ADM. 51-905 Log, *SHREWSBURY*
    h. A.O.-3. The Dunmore papers.
    i. C.O.-5 Official Correspondence Lord Germain

Many of these were readily available on micro-film through the Colonial Records project of the Virginia State Library. The ship's logs were researched for me, in London, by Lt. Cmdr. Charles Stuart, R.N. Ret.

2. The Clements Library, University of Michigan, Ann Arbor.
    a. The Clinton papers
    b. The Germain papers

3. The Huntington Library, San Marino, Calif.
    a. The L'Aine Log Book: HM 551
    b. The Joseph Juenot Log Book HM 578

4. Massachusetts Historical Society, Boston.
    The papers of Henry Knox.

5. Virginia State Library, Richmond.
    a. Calendar of Virginia State Papers.
    b. Official letters... Governors of Virginia.

6. The Mariner's Museum Library, Newport News, Va.
    An outstanding collection of prints and maps.

7. The Newberry Library, Chicago, Ill.
    The Graves Scrapbook.

In addition, several collections published in book form:

8. The Writings of George Washington, ed by Jared
   Sparks. 12 vols., Boston, 1834

9. The Graves Papers and Other Documents. French
   Chadwick. Naval Historical Society, N.Y., 1916

10. Letters Written by Sir Samuel Hood
    Navy Records Society. London, 1895

11. Operations of the French Fleet Under Comte
    de Grasse, in 1781–82. John D.G. Shea, 1864

12. Admiral de Grasse and American Independence.
    by Charles Lewis. Naval Institute 1945

13. The Naval Campaign of Comte De Grasse During
    the American Revolution, 1781–83by Karl G.
    Tornquist. Trans. A. Johnson, 1942

14. Rochambeau; A Commemoration...
    by, DeB. Randolph Keim. U.S. G.P.O. 1907

15. Diary of Frederick Mckenzie,1775–81
    Cambridge,MA. 1930

16. The Correspondence of George Washington and
    Comte de Grasse. Scott, Brown. G.P.O. 1931

17. The Virginia Campaign and the Blockade and Seige
    of Yorktown, 1781. H.L. Landers. G.P.O. 1931.

18. The North Carolina State Records, Raleigh, N.C.

19. Memories of the War in The Southern Dept.
    Henry Lee, 1828. Rev. R.E. Lee, 1869

(For additional information on quotes
contact the author in care of publisher.)

FOREWORD

When the first settlers stepped ashore at Jamestown in Virginia, they undoubtedly carried the seeds of the War For Independence, or American Revolution, in their hearts. Although those seeds took over 165 years to burst into bloom, they were certainly planted early and nurtured over those years.

The process is somewhat analogous to raising a child to the point where you send them off to college. It is then that the flower of independence begins to unfold. Although the parents continue to furnish nourishment, the spirit of independence grows. Distance from home, differences in physical and social environment, and changes in life style bring the need, and demand, for local input into the regulations and guide-lines for local activities. If the parents listen and understand the message, and adjust to the demand for a change in relationship, a stronger, long lasting one develops---if not, sooner or later, REBELLION, and a fractured familial situation.

In the middle 1700s, few of the men of the "ruling class" in England wanted to listen to, much less try to understand, the message from the colonies--what the colonials wanted was a larger voice in the government of their part of the empire---not separation. Whenever any one of those few who did understand raised his voice in Parliament, or elsewhere, he spoke to deaf ears. To make matters worse the demands on England, from her troubled empire, coupled with harassment from her European neighbors, far exceeded her abilities to handle all the problems. In addition, the British government, army, and navy were rife with political infighting and cronyism. In the halls of government, knowledge, experience, and ability were less important than noble connection.

In 1775 REBELLION broke out in the colonies!

In telling this story of the final days of the Revolution, I have chosen to present the events, decisions, and conflicts through the words of the participants, with a few observations here and there. This approach comes from a statement made by Professor J.A.Froude, of Oxford University, in 1872:

"If you would understand a particular period, study the original authorities: go to the chronicles written by men who lived at the time and breathed the contemporary air---drink at the fountain. Read if you can find them, the letters and writings of the persons you are concerned with---take nothing second-hand."

Only occasionally have I substituted a word or phrase for the sake of modern-day clarity. It has been an interesting adventure.

PROLOGUE

High Noon, September 5, 1781! Gulls wheeling in the sky over the entrance of Chesapeake Bay were treated to a sight rarely seen by sea-faring men: forty three sailing men-of-war, 19 British, 24 French, about to engage in one of the most important naval battles in American history. Why here? Why now? What brought these ships to Virginia's shores? And how did a British admiral's pique affect the outcome?

To understand how and why the culmination of our War For Independence came to Virginia and the Chesapeake Bay, and to appreciate the significance of the Battle Off The Capes of Virginia, we must turn the calendar back. We must go back to the bombardment and burning of Norfolk town on January 1, 1776: an act of reprisal from Virginia's last Royal Governor before fleeing the colony. We must go back to the May 1779 invasion of Hampton Roads by forces under Admiral George Collier and Gen. Edward Matthews. Back to the invasion led by that turncoat general, Benedict Arnold in December 1780; and finally the last one, led by Lt. General Earl Charles Cornwallis.

It would also do well to look at the personalities of some of the major military figures who took part:

ON THE AMERICAN SIDE:

General George Washington, Commander in Chief of Allied Forces. A born leader, he kept his forces loyal and in the field in spite of unbelievable hardships. Although well organized, he was still capable of innovation if circumstances called for it. He could come to a decision in a short time. Although he was a native Virginian, He did not plan for, or expect, the final engagements of the War for Independence to occur in Virginia. His plan was to attack and take the British stronghold of New York city and its environs.

Major-General Marquis Joseph Paul Gilbert de Lafayette, a young French nobleman, wise beyond his years. He volunteered his services to Washington in the early days of the war. The relationship between the two became very close and endured the rest of their lives. A natural-born leader, his troops loved him and followed him all through the back country of Virginia and finally to Yorktown. He was also very instrumental in getting French support, financial and military, for the American cause.

General Jean Baptist Comte de Rochambeau, leader of the French land forces. He brought three regiments of troops when he joined Washington at Newport, R.I. in July of 1780. At age 55 he came with considerably more military experience than Washington, and his troops were "regular army"; but, he had no problems with serving under Washington as Commander-in-Chief. He was knowledgeable, but with no air of superiority, in fact amiable. He well understood the state of the American Army. Rochambeau and Washington worked very well together.

Admiral Francois Joseph Paul Comte de Grasse, With a long naval career which included several battles with British fleets, DeGrasse, 10 years older than Washington, came to the Chesapeake with a reputation for being a hard-driving commanding officer, but somewhat cautious. His operations were generally "by the book"; however, if he had not been adaptive in his plans, after the Battle Off The Capes, the siege of Yorktown might have ended differently.

ON THE BRITISH SIDE;

Lord George Germain, Minister of War, was not the best of the leaders of the British government at the time. He got his position because he favored the King's policy of "rule or ruin". He never understood the message from the colonies. He was poor at communicating and in planning and carrying out strategy, but still insisted on butting in on field operations. He played favorites and did not like Sir Henry Clinton.

General Sir Henry Clinton, Commander-in-Chief: A reluctant commanding officer who had asked to be allowed to resign on several occasions. Although knighted by King George III, he was not of the Nobility and his writings indicate he was self-conscious of this. Clinton was cautious, a stand-patter who believed in holding what he had rather than risk trying to conquer more. He was slow to reach decisions and not very forceful. His overall strategy for the war was to control the ports and commerce in order to starve the Rebels into submission.

In 1779, he was given his second-in-command, Lt. Gen. Earl Charles Cornwallis, by Lord George Germain, Minister of War. At first pleased with his second, in a little over a year Clinton thought he was uncontrollable. He grew to dislike both of those men.

Lt. General Earl Charles Cornwallis, Second-in-Command, and commander of the southern forces. Britian's most aggressive general, forceful, headstrong, hungry for military advancement and independent command. In 1779 he returned to the colonies as second-in-command. He was effusive in his praise of Gen. Clinton and his happiness to serve under him. In a little over a year this changed. Being of "the nobility", he had the ear of Lord George Germain and corresponded directly with him---by-passing his superior, Gen. Clinton. Cornwallis failed to understand that the occupation of enemy strong-holds was as important to suppressing the rebellion as conquest: his southern campaign accomplished little, strategically.

Two more Generals are quoted frequently in this story, but as they were under the command of Gens. Clinton and Cornwallis, their decisions were not critical to the outcome of the final stages of the war. However, one, Brig. Gen. Benedict Arnold, rates a few words.

Brig. Gen. Benedict Arnold; the hero of Saratoga and the black-guard of West Point. Arnold was an outstanding field general, brave and bold, recognized by both sides for his expertise. Arnold believed that the citizens of the colonies, who were not loyal to the King, were enemies. He felt they should know and feel the presence of his army.

Admiral Sir George Rodney; Rodney entered the navy in his early youth as a Captain's boy. He was intelligent and self-confident; a good naval tactician, but with a quick temper. He was also known as a heavy gambler, usually in debt. Named commanding officer of the Leeward Islands in October 1779, one of the reasons for his raid on the previously neutral Dutch port of St. Eustatius was to solve his gambling debts: as commanding officer, he was entitled to a per centage of the value of all prizes taken.

Admiral Sir Samuel Hood was sent to the Leeward Islands Command as Second to Admiral Rodney., shortly after the St. Eustatius raid. Having know each other for years, the two professed admiration for each other; but, like Clinton and Cornwallis, this soon changed to antipathy. In July of 1781, Rodney turned over command of the fleet to Adm. Hood with instructions to take his 14 ships to New York to join forces with the North Atlantic squadron to seek out the French fleet. On arrival at New York, with his 14 ships to join the 7 stationed there, Hood heard of Admiral Arbuthnot's early departure. Apparently he thought he would assume command of the combined fleet: to his chagrin, he found that Admiral Thomas Graves had one year seniority over him, making Graves the new Commander. On learning this, Hood seemed to develop a state of umbrage which lasted for sometime.

Admiral Thomas Graves; 67, took command of the North Atlantic fleet when he was past his prime. His appointment was temporary pending arrival of Admiral Digby. Graves was overly cautious and never in a hurry. He and Clinton were so sure the French fleet was coming to New York that the precariousness of Cornwallis' situation at Yorktown did not strike them.

* * * * *

We also have to understand the importance of Virginia, strategically located in the middle of the thirteen colonies, with large rivers and bays offering easy access to British Navy ships and American blockade runners. Virginia, most populous of the colonies and most fruitful in agricultural products. Interwoven with all this were the problems of communication--no phones, radios, planes, or autos, just couriers on horseback, or in "swift sailing vessels", both subject to the vagaries of weather and capture.

After all is said and done, fate as much as strategy played a key role in ending the war in Virginia

CHAPTER ONE

"... next operation....the Chesapeake!"

At quarter after three on the afternoon of January 1, 1776 a dreadful cannonading began to rain down on Norfolk town from three British ships anchored in the harbor. About seventy guns were involved. Firing continued for seven hours, uninterrupted, then slowing to intermittent, it continued until evening of the 3rd. Under cover of fire from the ships, British troops landed and set fire to houses and warehouses along the waterfront. At one time, the troops got their field pieces into the streets, but were beat back, with no injuries to patriot forces. The fires burned fiercely all night, through the next day, and were still burning on Wednesday. "The detested town of Norfolk is no more----only about 12 houses have escaped the flames." wrote a British midshipman.

"They have destroyed the largest town in Virginia: one of three which carried on a trade. They have done their worst, with no other result than to harden our resolve and force us to lay aside our childish fondness for Britain and foolish dependence on her. We have long borne the oppression of ungenerous trade restrictions....calculated as badges of our subjection, and we have been too long content to just refuse to purchase commodities taxed for no purpose except to raise a revenue in America. Our patience and moderation served only to encourage them to proceed to greater lengths---and now, Norfolk is no more!" (Vol. 4, series 4 Force's **American Archives**) So ended, you might say, the last official act of the last Royal Governor of Virginia, John Murray, Earl of Dunmore.

* * * * *

After the bombardment of Norfolk, Lord Dunmore took his small fleet into the Chesapeake, hopefully awaiting reinforcements, which never came.

On February 17th Gen. Sir Henry Clinton, second in command of British Land Forces in North America, stopped at the Chesapeake while on his way south to Wilmington, N.C.. In talks with Dunmore, Clinton gave his theory for winning the war: large scale land operations would not succeed because troops depended on water-borne resupply. "...you cannot go further into the country than your river is navigable to large ships." The Rebels should be controlled by a war of expedition, desultory raids from strongly held posts on navigable water. The best place for this---"the Chesapeake...that great station from which it all must start. It has many good harbors and navigable rivers."[10]

While at Wilmington, on March 23rd, Gen. Clinton wrote Commander-in-Chief, Gen. William Howe, in New York, "...I have had it as my constant opinion that the provinces bordering Chesapeake Bay, and the rivers flowing into it, were the most accessible of any part of the continent. Information received on my voyage down has confirmed it. Therefore, if I am not prevented by my instructions, my plans will be to send part of the troops to occupy a post on Perquimans River (Hertford, N.C.) and take the remainder to Virginia to establish a post on Nansemond River or on the Southeast Branch of Elizabeth River, where I shall possess Princess Anne and Norfolk Counties. There, protected by the totally impassable Dismal Swamp on the southwest, an asylum and rendezvous will be open to all desiring to join the King's Standard."[11]

* * * * *

At the same time Dunmore and Clinton were conferring, an enigmatic English soldier of fortune, Charles Lee, who had talked Congress into making him an American General, was sent to Virginia, by General George Washington, to organize the defense of Eastern Virginia. Later that year, Lee was captured by the British during the battle at Monmouth, N.J. Attempting to ingratiate himself with British General Howe, Lee offered a plan to end the Rebellion by gaining control of Chesapeake Bay and Eastern Virginia.

* * * * *

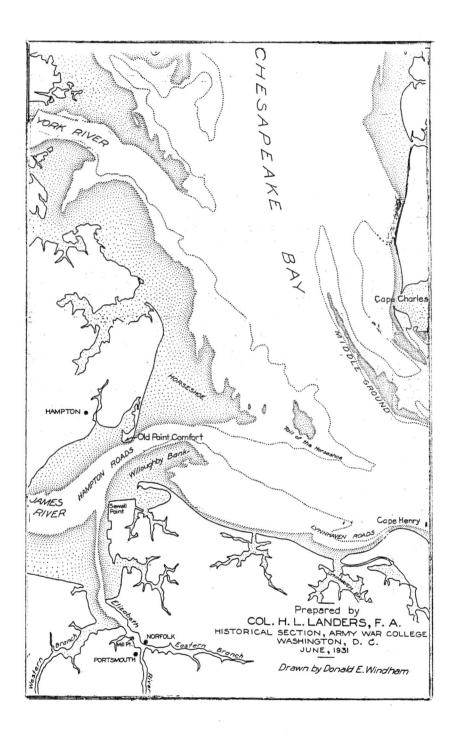

CHESAPEAKE BAY

YORK RIVER

Cape Charles

MIDDLE GROUND

HORSESHOE

HAMPTON

Old Point Comfort

Tail of the Horseshoe

HAMPTON ROADS

Willoughby Bank

JAMES RIVER

Sewell Point

LYNNHAVEN ROADS

Cape Henry

Elizabeth

NORFOLK

Mill Pt.

PORTSMOUTH

Western Branch

Eastern Branch

River

Lynnhaven Bay

Prepared by
COL. H. L. LANDERS, F. A.
HISTORICAL SECTION, ARMY WAR COLLEGE
WASHINGTON, D. C.
JUNE, 1931

Drawn by Donald E. Windham

Gen. Clinton became Commander-in-Chief, British Forces in North America in May 1778 when Gen. William Howe retired. His appointment was due in large part to his cousin the Duke of Newcastle, dispenser of political patronage. Although Clinton understood the situation in America, he was poorly equipped for the job, emotionally. He lacked self-confidence, was suspicious of the motives of superiors and subordinates, and lacked communication and leadership skills.

* * * * *

In May of '79, Commander in Chief Clinton sent Adm. George Collier and Gen. Edward Matthews to Virginia with orders "--to draw back to Virginia any Rebel troops sent south or westward, and prevent the march of any troops destined for Washington's army."[1] They were to destroy any ships and supply depots in Elizabeth and Nansemond Rivers, which the Rebels might use to supply their army in South Carolina.

After rampaging up and down those rivers, and torching ships and stores of naval supplies, Admiral Collier reported to General Clinton; "I am firmly of opinion it is essentially necessary for His Majesty's Service that this port of Norfolk remain in our hands. To me it is of more real consequence and advantage than any other Crown possession in America. By securing it, the trade of the Chesapeake would end, and the sinews of rebellion be destroyed! I trust you will give orders for reenforcement....so we may hold and improve the advantages we have acquired." [1]
Because of slow communication by sailing ship, Gen. Clinton's reply did not reach Collier in time to prevent the return of the expedition to New York.

Later that year, James Parker, a Loyalist who fled Norfolk with Lord Dunmore, now living in London, wrote General Matthews giving a detailed description of Tidewater and the people. He also opined on the advantages and disadvantages of Portsmouth and Yorktown: he thought Portsmouth the best location for a permanent post. This information was offered in anticipation of another expedition to Hampton Roads.

* * * * *

At the same time, on the American side, Commander in Chief General Washington, wrote General Lafayette, who had temporarily returned to France, saying he would welcome him back at the head of a gallant French Corps or as Major General of an American Corps. Lafayette received this in January 1780. He took it to mean the Americans would welcome a French Expeditionary Force and set out to get one!

In February 1780, French Foreign Minister Vergennes notified Lafayette that a decision had been made to send an Expeditionary Force, commanded by Comte de Rochambeau, to America. Lafayette should return to America post haste and resume his position of Major General in the American Army. He was to advise Gen. Washington that six ships-of-the-line, under Admiral de Ternay, and a 6000 man Corps, under Rochambeau, would sail in the spring. Although they were ordered to Rhode Island, provisions should also be made to receive them at the Chesapeake.

The French Frigate Hermoine, with Lafayette and staff onboard, slipped out of LaRochelle harbor on March 14th bound for America: She arrived at Newport, R.I. April 28th. Lafayette found American army morale and conditions low. A Committee of Congress had reported; "...the patience of the soldiery who have endured every conceivable hardship, and borne it with fortitude and perseverance, beyond expectation, is on the point of being exhausted." Lafayette, because of concern for negative reactions in Paris, decided not to advise Vergennes of this. It wasn't until May 10th that Lafayette finally sat down with Gen. Washington and told him of the French Expedition. Immediately, Washington began planning for an attack on New York.

* * * * *

In May of 1780, Gen. Clinton, led a combined naval and army force, in a siege of Charleston. The American Forces, which included a contingent of Virginians under General William Woodford, hero of the 1776 defense of Norfolk, capitulated on the 12th.

Shortly, Gen. Clinton instructed Lt. General Cornwallis, who was assuming command of Southern Operations, "....as communications will be precarious, I think it necessary to tell Your Lordship my plans, of which you are likely to bear a part. You know part of my plan was to go into Chesapeake Bay; but, I am apprehensive that information the Admiral and I received concerning the anticipated arrival of a French Fleet may make it necessary for him to take his fleet to New York, in which case, I shall also go there."

"When Your Lordship has finished your campaign, I wish you to assist in operations planned for the Chesapeake, as soon as we are free of worries of a superior fleet and the season will permit. This should be in September or early October. I am convinced this should not be attempted without a great naval force. I do not believe a great land force is needed. I propose Your Lordship meet the Admiral at the Chesapeake. Our first objective should be taking post at Norfolk or Suffolk, or near Hampton Roads––– then proceed up the Chesapeake to Baltimore. **The only thing in which we all agree is that our next operation must be in the Chesapeake."** [16] (auth. emphasis)

* * * * *

The promised French fleet of Admiral de Ternay, seven ships-of-the-line, two frigates, two cutters, and thirty two transports, arrived in Newport. R.I. July 11th. Onboard were 5000 troops under General Comte de Rochambeau. Two days later, a British fleet, under Admiral Thomas Graves, anchored at New York.

* * * * *

On August 23rd, Cornwallis wrote Gen. Clinton, "..my actions will depend on operations your Excellency may think proper to pursue in the Chesapeake, which appears to me, next to the security of New York, one of the most important objects of the war." [17]

Shortly thereafter, General Clinton wrote Gen. Cornwallis, "...I have always thought operations in Chesapeake of great importance; and, often discussed with Admiral Arbuthnot, the necessity of a diversion there in your Lordship's favor; but, until now, have

not been able, to obtain a convoy for that purpose. I
have written Admiral Sir George Rodney of my wishes
to send an expedition there. He has agreed to give
every naval assistance. It will be dispatched in a few
days. Soon after, Clinton instructed General Alexander
Leslie; "...proceed with your command to Chesapeake
Bay: on arrival, pursue such measures you judge most
likely to suit the purpose of this expedition: the
primary objective is to make a diversion in favor of
Lt. Gen. Earl Cornwallis. I believe it would be best to
go up James River, as high as possible, seize or
destroy any stores of provisions the enemy may have
at Petersburg or Richmond, finally, to establish a post
on Elizabeth River. The direction of every operation is
submitted to Earl Cornwallis--". [14]

* * * * *

Near this time, in New York, The American turncoat, Benedict Arnold, was welcomed by British Commander in Chief Clinton and given the rank of
Brigadier General of the Provisional troops.

* * * * *

Reacting to increased British activity, Virginia
Governor Jefferson wrote Samuel Huntington, President
of Congress, on September 14th, "...that the enemy
thinks of taking Portsmouth in the way they give out,
does not seem probable. ...that they think of taking
possession of it at all, seems quite unlikely, while it is
in the power of our Allies to send a superior fleet into
Chesapeake Bay, to which theirs would fall prey." [15]

At Portsmouth, October 12th, Col. John Christian
Senf, A Danish engineer serving under Gen. Horatio
Gates, wrote Gates of an inspection he made of
Yorktown, Hampton, and Portsmouth; "...York, consist-
ing of about 50 houses, is a very defensible spot, by
water as by land, if proper use is made of it. There
is not less than six fathoms of water from Cape Henry
to York with good Navigation. ...Gloucester, about
three-quarters of a mile across the river, has good
high ground on both sides. Above those points, the
river broadens, and ships-of-the-line may go 8 or 9

miles up and lay in safety. (L'Enfant, a French 74, lay there last winter). Troops may be quartered there more easily than anywhere near Hampton Roads. Hampton has about 40 houses. It is defended by a small bar which no ship drawing more than 7 feet can get over: the enemy could land above or below and take it."

"the 11th, we crossed Hampton Roads, went up Elizabeth River, where no large ships can lay, to Portsmouth, with about 25 houses, the rest were burnt in '79. Norfolk, across the river, was an extensive place, but was burnt down in 1776: about 15 houses are rebuilt. The fort is destroyed except for four guns remounted to prevent privateers from doing mischief. There are no soldiers except a few militia....". [14]

Senf also told of intelligence from a Capt. Lewis, newly arrived from St Eustatia, Dutch West Indies; a French frigate had reported that Count D'Estaing sailed from Brest on the sixth of August with 26 ships-of-the- line and 90 transports.

Writing from Hall's Mill, near Portsmouth, on October 22nd, Militia Gen. Thomas Nelson advised Governor Jefferson: "...this morning I was informed the enemy had landed at Lynnhaven Bay. A party of light horse, after taking possession of Kemps Landing, were on their way to the Great Bridge. The cattle that were collected in Princess Anne County, for the Commissary, have fallen into enemy hands. ...I suppose they intend to make their winter quarters in this state." [54]

In Williamsburg, Gov. Jefferson wrote Gen. Washington, "...it is mortifying that a people able and zealous to contend with the enemy, should be reduced to fold their arms for lack of means of defense. Of the troops we are able to collect, not a single man has ever seen the enemy." [55]

From Hampton, James Innes wrote Jefferson, "...I think I know the disposition of the people of the lower country. Their attachment to the cause is as unanimous and firm as any class of people on the continent; but, the extremely exposed situation of their properties and families, and fear of captivity or famine, may act so strongly upon them in the hour of alarm and danger---as to produce a languor and indecision totally incompatible with the rapid ...movements of war. The feelings of the man may, in a fatal moment, swallow up the sentiments of the patriot. ...During my experience in the Northern Army, I learned one truth, no aid of militia could be drawn from the part of the country being invaded."[55]

The Virginia Gazette for that week reported, "...On the 20th, a British fleet of 54 ships, 25 of which are large, arrived in Chesapeake Bay. On the 23rd, 1000 troops landed at Newport News, marched to Hampton and took possession."

The same week, Gen. Nathaniel Greene, heading south to relieve Gen. Gates, wrote Gen. Washington suggesting that if Gen. Rochambeau and Admiral deTernay would embark the French troops at Newport and go to the Chesapeake, they might catch the British by surprise, and render a deadly blow.

* * * * *

Oct. 24th, onboard H.M.S. *ROMULUS*, in Hampton Roads, Gen. Leslie wrote Gen. Cornwallis; "I am ordered to put myself under Your Lordship's command. From intelligence I get, I don't hear of your being nearer than Camden, S.C. Sir Henry thought you had come into North Carolina. ...I do not believe it advisable to attempt to join you until I know your situation."[11]

On Nov. 6, Clinton wrote Cornwallis of Leslie's 2500 man expedition to the Chesapeake:----Leslie was under his orders: "...if his instructions are not as you approve, Your Lordship may alter them as you please." He also discussed problems of reenforcing any action in Virginia. "..as soon as I know of Your Lordship's determination to keep post at Portsmouth, I will consider what additional forces I can spare. With superiority at sea, I might possibly send 2000 more for winter operation."[11] Clinton saw Virginia operations as "desultory expeditions" blocking the Chesapeake, and, by commanding the James, halting the flow of forces and supplies southward. "..as I have often said, except as a visitor, I shall not move to the Chesapeake unless Washington goes there in force, which he doesn't seem inclined to do."[18]

Gen. Clinton wrote Lord Germaine again on Nov. 10th, "...By all the copies of Lord Cornwallis' letters sent your Lordship, you will observe he recommends a diversion in the Chesapeake as essential to success of his operations. By my first instruction to Major Gen. Leslie, Your Lordship will perceive I pointed this out as the principle object of his expedition. Wishing to guard against every possible embarrassment to Earl Cornwallis, I thought it proper to make an addition to those instructions; '....should that post at Portsmouth be occupied, I shall probably send all of the troops I can possibly spare from this army'....".[19]

From Portsmouth, Gen. Leslie advised Clinton that, at the request of Lord Rawdon, with Cornwallis in Carolina, he was taking his whole command to Cape Fear River, at Wilmington, N.C., to join Cornwallis. Clinton was beside himself: he now had 2500 fewer troops in his Northern army; but, felt he could not counter Cornwallis actions. He wrote a friend; "I will do all I can to recover from this blow...but, **this ends all Golden Dreams in the Chesapeake.**" (auth. emphasis)

By now, the reader should have detected Clinton's reluctant deference to Lord Cornwallis' plans. Earlier that year, upset with unpredictable Adm. Arbuthnot, Clinton wrote Lord Germaine, Secretary of North American Affairs, asking for Arbuthnot's removal, or offering his resignation. In early November he was advised Admiral Graves would replace Arbuthnot; if Clinton was still unhappy with his reenforcements, he might resign his command to Lord Cornwallis.

Near that time, Cornwallis wrote Leslie; "however painful and distressing my situation has been, and however dark the prospects, it cannot be supposed that, as a military man, I should not rather have command in the south than be third at New York."[19]

While off Cape Hatteras, Gen. Leslie wrote Lord George Germain, on November 12th;"...I must confess I left Portsmouth with some misgivings for it may be made a strong post and commands the lower country. It is the key to the wealth of Virginia".[11]

* * * * *

American Generals Greene and Steuben, on their way south, stopped in Virginia on November 16th. Seeing the confused state of affairs in the Virginia Militia, caused by the presence of Leslie's army, Greene left Steuben in command in Virginia.

Upset by field conditions he was seeing among the troops in the Carolinas, on December 6th, Nathaniel Greene wrote Governor Jefferson, "I find the troops in Gen. Gates command in wretched condition, destitute of anything necessary for the comfort or convenience of soldiers. It is impossible for men to render any service, even if well disposed, while starving with cold and hunger. YOUR troops may be said to be naked.... It is impossible to preserve discipline when troops want for everything: to attempt severity will only thin the ranks by more desertion."[11]

Much later, Thomas Jefferson wrote of the Virginia Militia of that time, "...they numbered 49,971 men, individually possessed of the raw qualities of which soldiers are made; but, collectively, the Virginia militia was unorganized, undisciplined, poorly armed, wasteful, and, militarily, unreliable. Gen. Steuben was faced with Continental troops who were sick from exposure, had little clothing or military equipment and would desert or refuse to re-enlist. He advised Gen. Greene he was better off without them.".[11]

* * * * *

In New York, on Dec. 13th, Clinton wrote Cornwallis, replying to his September letters (received Nov. 12), "...Wishing to give Your Lordship's operation in North Carolina every assistance. though I can ill spare it, I have sent another expedition to the Chesapeake under Brig. Gen. Arnold, and Lt. Cols. Dundas and

Simcoe. The force is not equal to General Leslie's, but, I trust it will operate essentially in favor of Your Lordship; either by striking Greene's Petersburg depot or by taking post at Portsmouth, which I have ever considered very important, for reasons most obvious. If we take post there and fortify and assemble the inhabitants, it ought not afterwards be quitted. ...."

"I must tell Your Lordship, these detachments leave me very bare of troops, and Washington continues very strong, with at least 12,000 men. He has yet to detach a single man to the southward. ...there are 6,000 French troops already in Rhode Island, and six more regiments are expected. As I have said before, I think Your Lordship's movements in the South most important, and, as I have always done, I will continue to give all the assistance I can. If we can hold the entrance of the Chesapeake, I don't think the rebels will attempt either province, Virginia or North Carolina. Should Your Lordship, at anytime, judge it expedient to reinforce the Corps under Brig. Gen. Arnold, either continue it under his orders or send any other General Officer you think proper, to take command...".[1]

The same day, in New York, Clinton gave orders to Brig. Gen. Benedict Arnold, who had gone over to the British in October, "..proceed with your command to the Chesapeake Bay: as soon as possible, establish a post at Portsmouth on Elizabeth River. Make known your intention of remaining there. Assemble and arm such of the people as you believe are well affected to His Majesty and are inclined to join you.

After establishing a post at Portsmouth, I would not have you make any excursions from there unless they can be made without the least danger to the safety of that post, which is always to be considered the primary object of your expedition. Should Lord Cornwallis require any cooperation from you before that is done, you are directed to obey his commands; but, after you have established the post at Portsmouth, my request is that you do not undertake any operation with the least risk to that station--- unless Earl Cornwallis should positively direct."[2]

Arnold's ships ran into a severe gale off Virginia's Eastern Shore on Dec. 26th---and separated. They reassembled in Hampton Roads. On the 31st, Arnold transferred his troops to smaller boats and started up the James towards Richmond.

CHAPTER TWO:

Bring off this greatest traitor:

On January 2, 1781, Governor Jefferson wrote General Steuben, "...I received word of the arrival in the Bay of a hostile fleet of 19 ships and 10 sloops of war. The advance guard was at Warrasqueak Bay, on the James, near Smithfield, yesterday. According to some deserters, their destination is Petersburg."[55]

Arnold's flotilla anchored at Westover, Col. William Byrd's estate, on the 4th, disembarked troops in a heavy rain and marched for Richmond, arriving next morning. The Queen's Rangers, under Lt. Col. John Graves Simcoe, marched on to Westham, where they destroyed one of the finest cannon foundaries in America. Gov. Jefferson wrote Washington that they also burnt the boring mill and magazine; and threw six tons of powder into the James River.

Years later, Issac Hennings, a Jefferson slave, reminisced about the British actions in Richmond; "...day fore British came, Mr. Jefferson sent his family off in a carriage...took his spy-glass and git up in the sky-light window of the palace, towards Williamsburg. 'Fore the British fired, Richmond folk thought they was Petersburg militia coming to help. ...soons they fired, not a white man was seen in Richmond. ...When they fired, master told John to fetch his horse Caractacus, and rode off. ...when the British came, officer asked, 'where's the Governor?' Issac's father said, 'gone to the mountains!' British said....didn't want to hurt him, only...put some silver hand-cuffs on him!" (Memories of a Monticello Slave)

* * * * *

January 9th, Gen. Washington wrote Gen. Steuben, in Virginia, "...I am sorry to inform you of a general mutiny in the Pennsylvania line, which took place the night of the 1st. They marched off with their arms and artillery, declaring they were going to Congress for a redress of their grievances."[1]

* * * * *

In New York, Lt. Frederick McKenzie diaried; "Jan. 7th; we have great hopes the loyalists of Maryland and the southern provinces, hearing of the mutiny of the Pennsylvania troops, will rise up and declare themselves. There is little doubt they will if Lord Cornwallis has successed in Carolina and Arnold has established himself in Virginia. Arnold wrote Clinton he did not destroy private stores and vessels around Richmond and Petersburg because he felt they were owned by people well affected to His Majesty".[15]

At Richmond, the British reembarked on the 10th and started back down the James: on the 11th, they were near City Point (Hopewell), the 13th at Williamsburg. On the 14th, they disembarked at Harding's Ferry and marched to Smithfield. The 17th, they were at Mackie's Mill where they dislodged some Rebel troops commanded by Col. Josiah Parker. Col. Simcoe's Queen's Rangers marched ahead to Sleepy Hole on Nasemond River, then into Portsmouth on the 19th. The rest of Arnold's army arrived on the 20th; "to the great joy of the inhabitants", said Gen. Arnold, in a letter to Clinton. He attributed a great deal of his success to "the industry, and knowledge of a Loyalist privateer, Capt. William Goodrich, former resident of Portsmouth, who left with Dunmore in '76".[16]

* * * * *

Assessing his situation, on Jan. 15th, General Washington, in Conn., wrote Lt. Col. John Laurens, at Philadelphia, who was about to embark for France, "...to me, it appears evident, that:
1st...considering the duffused population of the states, the difficulty of drawing their resources together, the temper of part of the inhabitants, the want of a sufficient stock of national wealth as a foundation for revenue, and the almost total extinction of commerce; the efforts we have been compelled to

make, for carrying on the war, have exceeded the abliities of this country: ---and by degrees, brought it to a crisis which renders immediate and effectual assistance from abroad indispensible to our safety."...

"6thly:...the patience of the army, from an almost uninterrupted series of distresses, is near exhaustion; ...you are well acquainted with their sufferings, for want of clothing, provisions, and want of pay..."

"8thly:...that from the foregoing considerations, comes the absolute necessity of an immediate and effective supply of money, large enough to be a foundation for substantial arrangements of finance, revive public credit, and give vigor to our operations."

"9thly: ...next to a loan of money, a constant naval superiority on our coast is most interesting. This would reduce the enemy to a difficult defensive. ...indeed, it is inconceivable how they could subsist a large force in this country if we commanded the seas."

"10th:...an additional supply of troops is extremely desirable. Besides a reenforcement in numbers, the excellence of the French troops now here, with their perfect discipline and order, proves the great value of an addition to the corps."[1]

By early January, Gen. Steuben had collected a couple of thousand Virginia militia on the outskirts of Portsmouth. He also had a number of North Carolina militia, under General Gregory, available at the Great Bridge and the Northwest Bridge. Steuben called a conference of his officers and asked if they thought their troops might force Arnold to quit Portsmouth--- they answered no! They might be able to keep him in Portsmouth or slow him down if he came out again.

On Jan. 19th, at Smithfield, Col. Robert Lawson, Surry militia, wrote Steuben, "...why should Arnold march to Portsmouth when he could go much easily by water. ...I think it is plain, he means it as a decoy to draw us down as far as possible...and enable

him more easeily to effect his main objective, which is
certain to be a junction with Cornwallis and Leslie,
who by then will make a rapid push to here."[5a]

Jan. 22nd, Washington, in Newport, wrote Gen.
Robert Howe, of the North Carolina Continentals; "take
command of the detachment ordered to march against
the New Jersey mutineers ...compel them to uncon-
ditional submission, ...grant no terms while they have
arms in their hands, in a state of resistance. ...if you
succeed in compelling them to surrender, you will
immediately execute a few of the most active and
incendiary leaders!"[5] ---two were shot January 26.

* * * * *

On the 23rd Arnold, in Portsmouth, advised
Clinton, "...the line of works begun for the defense of
this place...are very extensive, and cannot be con-
tracted. ...Lt. Cols. Dundas and Simcoe agree with me,
that three thousand men are necessary for their
defense. We have all been greatly deceived by the
nature of the ground. ...as they are, the works are
of no service; and all our force cannot complete them
in three months. I think it my duty to request a reinforcement of at least two thousand men, which would
render this post permanent and secure it against any
force the country might bring against it." [5a]

* * * * *

The 31st, Gov. Jefferson wrote Gen. Muhlenburg,
now in Virginia, "As you are acquainted with the
treason of Arnold, I need say nothing more on it: ...I'm
sure you will agree it is very desirable to drag him
from under the wing of those who now shelter him.
...Having confidence in the men from the western side
of the mountains, as soon as they arrive, I want to
get that venture before a chosen few. ...your knowledge of them, and my confidence in your discretion,
induces me to ask you to pick proper ones among
them, as many as you think best, reveal our desire,
and engage them to undertake to seize and bring off
this greatest of all traitors!" ...If successful, they
shall receive five thousand guineas among them." [5b]

The same day, in New York, Lt. McKenzie entered in his diary, "...Arnold is bold, daring, and prompt in executing what he undertakes. I am almost sorry, for the British Generals, that such a man as he should have executed, with an inferior force, what a British General did not even attempt with a superior one."[15]

Down in the Caribbean, Admiral George Rodney, sailed the British West Indies fleet, into the previously regarded neutral Dutch port of St. Eustatius and captured 138 French, Spanish, and American ships loaded with goods, and over 2,100,000 pieces of eight. This action would prove crucial to the outcome of the Battle Off the Capes of Virginia.

* * * * *

In the western part of North Carolina, rays of sunlight were popping through the clouds of gloom that had stalked the Americans for a long time. General Nathaniel Green, after relieving Gates, though retreating, was doing a much better job of harassing Cornwallis. Cornwallis, abandoning his officers' baggage wagons, was pushing after Greene---extending his supply lines dangerously, as he moved deeper into hostile territory. Gen. Daniel Morgan had beaten British Col. Banestra Tarleton in a heated brawl.

Virginia Militia General Edward Stevens wrote Gov. Jefferson complaining of the militia: "...to my great mortification and astonishment, scarce a man would agree to stay to wait for Green. ....if the salvation of the country had depended on their staying ten or fifteen days, I don't believe they would have done it. MILITIA WONT DO! Their goal is to rub through their tour of duty with whole bones. ...I was obliged, by compulsion, to detain them for a day."[56]

Years later, Col. Henry Lee, of Lee's Partisan Legion, said of that period, "....when we add the comfort-less condition of our troops in point of clothing, rigors of the season, inclemency of the weather, our short supply of ammunition, and shorter supply of provisions, ...we have abundant cause to honor the soldier whose mental resources smoothed every difficulty and ultimately made good a retreat of 230 miles---unaided, except, occassionally by small corps of friendly militia, without the loss of either troops or stores. ...their shoes were generally worn out, body clothes much tattered, and not more than a blanket for four men. ...the single meal allowed us was always scanty, though good in quality and very nutritious, being bacon and corn meal."[15]

Writing of the same conditions, Col. William Davies, Commissary of Supply, wrote Gov. Jefferson, "...many men have not a remnant of clothing larger than a good napkin to cover their nakedness; a number of these depend upon others for a part of a blanket to shelter them at night from the cold. ...some of them are so naked they have refused furloughs to go home to try to get clothes, being ashamed, as well as unable to travel at this season." [16]

* * * * *

In Connecticut, Gen. Washington wrote French General Rochambeau, "...by recent accounts from Virginia, Arnold has left the James and marched to Portsmouth. ...If Mr. Destouches now has a superiority in force, as a result of the recent storm which damaged several British ships at New York, which would make it suitable to act, your Excellency may think Arnold's detatchment a worthy objective." [17]

On February 9th, Admiral Destouches dispatched Admiral de Tilly, in a 64 gun ship and two frigates, to the Chesapeake to attempt an action against Arnold; however, Rochambeau, wanting secrecy, did not advise Washington of this until three days later. As soon as Washington heard, he sent Lafayette and a Corps off to Virginia. Theodorick Bland, Virginia Delegate to Congress in Philadelphia, hearing of the move from French Ambassador Lucerne, wrote Gov. Jefferson on the 9th urging him to have pilots available at Cape Henry when the French arrived. Jefferson did not get this message until two days after their arrival.

At the same time, Gen. Steuben was trying to surround Arnold's post at Portsmouth: Gen. Issac Gregory, of the North Carolina Militia, reported he had 200 troops at the Northwest Bridge, below Great Bridge, and was expecting more. Paul Loyall, former Mayor of Norfolk, and Col. John Thorogood, of Princess Anne, took their militia to join Gregory. Gen. Muhlenberg reported Col. Mead was at Sleepy Hole in Nansemond County, Col. Mathews at Jericho, Col. Parker at Suffolk, and Col. Lawson near Smithfield.

* * * * *

From headquarters at Portsmouth, Gen. Benedict Arnold, trying to clean-up Princess Anne County, dispatched Col. Simcoe with 400 Queens Rangers to Kemp's Landing to find Capt. Amos Weeks, who was harassing the British anywhere he could find them.

Four days later, Arnold wrote Clinton of a plan to send 400 or 500 men, in boats, to Currituck Sound and down to the Albermarle to sweep them clean, then on to Edenton and New Bern to destroy shipping, and act as a diversion in favor of Lord Cornwallis.

* * * * *

Feb. 10th, in Connecticut, Gen. Washington wrote. Gen. Henry Knox, Commander of Continental Artillery, "...in a conference with Gen. Rochambeau, it was agreed that if, with the aid of our allies, we can have a naval superiority through the next campaign, and an army of 30,000 men....early enough in the season to operate in this quarter, it is incumbent upon us to make every preparation for the seige of New York, as far as funds and means make practicable. Application has already been made to the Court of France for a good supply of powder, arms, and cannon.

...In your calculations, estimate our forces at about 20,000. The rest, with proper siege and field apparatus, will be furnished by our allies. You are well acquainted with New York...therefore, you judge the means required for its reduction by siege. If we find ourselves unable to undertake this more capital expedition; and, we have the means, our secondary object, would be the reduction of Charleston.....".

CHAPTER THREE.

....Send more troops!

From Weathersfield, Conn., Washington wrote Rochambeau, on Feb. 15th, replying to his of the 3rd, "...it appears to have been your Excellency's expectation that Adm. Destouches would either go with his whole fleet, or send a detatchment, to Chesapeake Bay in quest of Arnold. ...there are a number of positions where Arnold, by putting his ships under protection of land batteries, may defy a naval attack....Portsmouth being one. ...Unless the ships have the good fortune to fall in with him embarked and moving from one place to another, they will have little prospect of success."[1] Washington was unaware that ships larger than frigates could not get up the Elizabeth---as British Adm. Collier had discovered in May 1779.

"...From these considerations, if the objective is sufficiently important, it is, in my opinion, essential there should be a cooperation of land and naval forces---and Mr. Destouches should protect the expedition with his whole fleet. Anticipating his thinking it advisable, and that Your Excellancy would approve a cooperation with part of your army, I sent a detatchment of 1200 men to proceed to Head of Elk River (top of Chesapeake Bay)...there to embark and proceed to cooperate. I did not delay until I could hear from Mr. Destouches and you, as there was not a moment to lose. ...they should arrive in about four weeks. ....if the Chevalier and you approve the project, ...it would be desirable if you could embark about 1000 troops on the ships, and as many pieces of artillery and apparatus as you think proper to spare. ....The capture of Arnold and his detatchment will be an event particularly agreeable to this country."[1]

Unfortunately, again, because of slow communications, another important letter arrived too late.

* * * * *

That same day, Gen. Arnold wrote Cornwallis of the arrival, in Lynnhaven Bay, of three French men-of-war. ....he hoped the arrival of the King's ships in Charleston would enable Commodore Gayton to bring a force superior to the French. Gayton sailed in the *ROMULUS*, on February 9th, convoying transports to Arnold. Arnold also wrote Gen. Lawson, of the Virginia Militia, at Suffolk, offering to exchange several prisoners taken during raids on Richmond and Petersburg, for Lt. Col. Jacob Elligood of His Majesty's Loyal American Regiment---the exchange was not approved.

Jacob Elligood was a long-time resident of Princess Anne County. When Lord Dunmore called for support in 1775, Elligood, and his brother-in-law John Saunders, were first to answer; gathering about 600 loyalists to join him. He was captured late in December '75 while fleeing to the Eastern Shore. He was an obstinate character who loved his native land, but would not foreswear his allegiance to his King. He was finally exchanged in the summer of 1781 and made his way to Cornwallis camp at Yorktown. Like most loyalists, he was banished from the colony. Unlike others who abandoned their lands and fled, Jacob insisted that his family remain on his estate throughout the war. Because of this, after the war, when the Virginia Legislature declared all abandoned lands escheated (forfeited) to the State, Elligood retained his ownership. Although Jacob never received permission to return to Virginia, his wife and children remained there, in possession, until the early 1800s.

* * * * *

From Hampton, Col. Dabney advised Gen. Steuben, on Feb. 14th, that a French 64 and two 36 gun frigates entered the Bay and anchored off Buckroe. They asked about the presence of British ships and the depth of Elizabeth River. Steuben swung into action; ordering Gen. Muhlenberg to prepare for an attack, Gen. Thomas Nelson to commandeer private boats to bring his militia across the James, and asked French Admiral de Tilley to bring his ships up the Elizabeth for use as siege guns. De Tilley said his 64 could not get up the river and the frigates would be insufficient: The grand plan died aborning. The 19th, Tilley weighed anchor and left, saying Adm. Destouches had instructed him not to remain longer than necessary: "...rest assured of my desire, on this occasion, to be useful to the United States of America."

One good thing did come from de Tilley's visit: outside the Capes, they captured the *ROMULUS* and a large brig. Onboard the brig were 159 former residents of the area, loyalists, hoping to return under the protection of Gen. Benedict Arnold.

From Richmond, on Feb. 16th, Gov. Jefferson advised Gen. Thomas Nelson, "...I am very anxious to prepare for cooperating with our allies and providing for their support: for that purpose, we suppose Yorktown the most effectual as an asylum for their vessels. Col Senf comes down with instructions. ..."[bb]

* * * * *

From New Windsor, Conn., Washington notified Lafayette to take command of the detachment being sent to Virginia: he was to cooperate with de Tilley's fleet, and Gen. Steuben. Their objective was to take Portsmouth and General Benedict Arnold. "...you are to do no act whatever with Arnold that directly or by implication may screen him from the punishment due his treason and desertion: if he should fall into your hands, you will execute it in the most summary way."[1]

On February 24th, Gov. Jefferson wrote Gen. Steuben, "...the nakedness of the militia at Williamsburg has almost produced a mutiny. ...you may judge from their temper what little prospect there is of your availing yourself of their aid on the south side of the James River, should you require it."[ii] It was said that in Gen. Muhlenberg's camp, ammunition was limited to eight rounds per man, and provisions for four days.

In Connecticut, Rochambeau wrote Washington on the 25th, "...letters found on the captured *ROMULUS* have decided M. Destouches to follow, at full, your

Excellency's plan, and to risk everything to hinder
Arnold from establishing himself at Portsmouth. He is
arming the *ROMULUS* and hopes that it, with his frigates, will be able to get up the Elizabeth. M.
Destouches will protect this expedition with his whole
fleet. ...I will send 1120 men...all my Grenadiers and
Chasseurs...commanded by Baron de Viomenil".[14]

* * * * *

Escorted by a company of Queen's Rangers,
General Benedict Arnold went to Kemp's Landing on
Feb. 21st. There he issued a proclamation calling on
the "good people of Princess Anne" to come in and
pledge their allegiance to His Majesty.

March 8th, from New York, Clinton wrote
Cornwallis, "...Admiral Arbuthnot seems to think the
whole, or a great part, of the French fleet at Newport
sailed for the Chesapeake on the 27th. He was ready
to sail at that time. I believe he has gone there, or
sent a sufficient force, to clear the Bay. Gen. Phillips
Corps is embarked and is at Sandy Hook awaiting the
Admiral. I am sure you know Phillip's instructions are
to cooperate with Your Lordship; therefore, please take
him under your orders until you hear further from
me."[14] With this move, Gen. Clinton had ensnared
himself a little deeper into the Chesapeake.

In London, on March 7th, Lord George Germain
wrote Lord Cornwallis, "...The reasons which you
assigned to calling Gen. Leslie from Virginia are
founded in wisdom, and could not fail being approved
by the King....I have no doubts Your Lordship will,
by this time, have had the honor to recover the
province of North Carolina for His Majesty. I am
optimistic enough to hope...the recovery of a part of
Virginia will crown your successes before the season
becomes too intemperate for land operations."[15]

* * * * *

March 6th, Col. Innes wrote Gov. Jefferson of
rumors from the enemy camp that Arnold and Col.
Dundas had a violent argument with Capt. Symonds of

the navy. Most of the British ships were anchored between Tucker's Mill (Hospital Point) and Gosport: Some were stationed near Craney Island, rigged for sinking, to prevent any attacking French ships from approaching near enough to Portsmouth to lay siege.

In the meantime, Lafayette, thwarted in his rendezvous with French ships at Head of the Elk, marched his troops to Annapolis. Leaving them there, he took a boat down the Bay to reconnoiter. On March 9th, Governor Jefferson addressed the House of Delegates, "...I think it my duty to advise the General Assembly of the refusal of considerable numbers of the militia of certain counties to come into the field, and the defiant departure of others, with their arms. These acts of disobedience to the laws may bring ill consequences. ...this suggests the need for some amendments to the invasion law, or you may wish to advise proper measures to be taken on this occasion."[55]

* * * * *

About this time, Gen. Steuben and Gov. Jefferson had a disagreement: Steuben accused Virginia of promising troops and equipment for the siege of Portsmouth, then not delivering. Jefferson replied he could only give orders---not execute them. He did give Steuben "impress power" to take horses and boats without compensation but, would not authorize the militia to help with the actual "impressing". Almost immediately, he countermanded himself, telling Steuben to return stud horses and breeding mares.

At the same time, Jefferson wrote Lafayette, "...mild laws, a people not used to war and prompt obedience, a want of the provisions of war and means of procuring them, often render our orders ineffectual, and oblige us to temporize...".[56] Jefferson could not seem to understand that he, himself, was a good part of his problem. His over-zealousness in protecting private property rights of the individual, and his opposition to "conscription for the duration" led to many frustrations on the part of those military men charged with defending the countryside.

In Newport, on March 11, 1781, Washington wrote Lafayette: "Dear Marquis: I informed you on the 8th that the French fleet had put to sea. The British fleet at New London did the same yesterday morning. I give you this notice lest you, upon hearing that a fleet had arrived below, might take for granted it was a friendly one and fall down to it. You will see that precaution is very necessary." S/ G. Washington"[1] The French fleet consisted of seven ship-of-the-line, the 44 gun *ROMULUS,* and some frigates. The British sailed with seven line-of-battle ships and a 50 gun frigate.

* * * * *

The March New York Gazette reported, "news from Virginia indicates Portsmouth is made a very formidable place...and is now secure against the united enterprises of France and Congress. ...Leading inhabitants of Princess Anne County, having been informed that General Arnold's intentions were to maintain a British garrison in their country, declared they would cooperate in all measures to drive out every man disaffected to His Majesty's government, and supply the King's troops with all sorts of provisions."

Writing to Major Gen. Phillips on March 10th, Gen. Clinton instructed, "Please proceed with the troops of your command to Chesapeake Bay, to form a junction with Brig. Gen. Arnold's corps, which you will take under your orders... The principle object of your expedition is the security of his troops. and the posts on Elizabeth River. Use every means to effect this end. If you find Arnold acting under orders from Lord Cornwallis, you will try to fulfill those orders. Make such movements with your corps as will most effectively assist His Lordship's operations."
"If the Admiral disapproves Portsmouth, saying he requires a fortified station for large ships in the Chesapeake, propose Yorktown or Old Point Comfort: if either can be acquired and maintained without great risk or loss, you are at liberty to take possession thereof. ....With regards to a station for the protection of the King's ships: I know of no place so proper as York, if it could be taken, fortified, and garrisoned

with 1000 men. ...if the heights of York and Gloucester cannot be well fortified, so as to render that post "hors d'insult" before the enemy can move a force against it, it may not be advisable to take it."

"Whenever the objects of this expedition are fulfilled, and you have strengthened the present works, you may return to New York" [1]

Clinton wrote Gen. Phillips again, on March 14th, advising that Admiral Arbuthnot, because of faulty intelligence, had lost an opportunity to give a "mortal blow" to the French at Newport. They had sailed in a snow storm: now Arbuthnot was hastening after them in his "copper-bottomed" ships. (which sailed faster because of the "anti-fouling" properties of copper) If Arbuthnot did not overtake the French at sea, Clinton did not foresee the French risking a fight in Lynnhaven Bay, but, rather take their fleet up river to Yorktown---which he had told the Admiral.

"... *Listen well to what I am saying!* ----I think if the French are gone to Chesapeake, they will shelter themselves in York River: the Admiral will immediately hold to his usual language---'he waits for the army'. That from South Carolina cannot come, as Colonel Balfour has, very injudiciously, sent home the transports. I cannot move a man until you send back the transports. If he proposes anything to you, he must first declare, *in writing, positively,* what his fleet will do, or at least attempt, before you can decide. After consulting with your officers, give me your opinion on what can be done and what land forces you will need to do it. If all agree that the French will be unattackable in a station at Yorktown, it must be blocked; then, we must do our best to assist Lord Cornwallis' operations. ....all must be settled in formal council---*Beware of verbal conversations! The Admiral will forget them and deny all he says!"* [1]

Initially, General Clinton never intended the Chesapeake to be a "major operation" but, after Adm. Collier..in '79, Gen. (Earl) Leslie...in '80, and Lord Cornwallis...'80-'81, had written Lord George Germain, Secretary for North American Affairs, saying how important it was, and Germain agreed, Clinton was caught in a dilemma: send more troops, against his better judgment, or risk the ire of Germain. On top of this, his second-in-command Cornwallis, who had the ear of London, had his own ideas of how the war should be run; as did Admiral Arbuthnot.

* * * * *

At the same time, in Yorktown, American Generals Lafayette and Steuben met to go over the planned operations against Arnold in Portsmouth, which would take place as soon as the French ships arrived.

In Hartford, Conn., George Washington wrote Massachusetts Governor Hancock, "...important operations expected to the southward, made it necessary for me to return to the North River. ...the success of the expedition now planned depends upon a naval superiority, and the force of the two fleets is so equal we must hope for, rather than entertain an assurance of victory. ....the army under my command is so reduced by the detachments I have made to cooperate with the French troops in Virginia, I am under the necessity of calling for the recruits raised in neighboring states."[1]

* * * * *

On the other side of the Atlantic at Brest, France, on March 14th, 1781, M. de Castinor, French Naval Secretary, called on Admiral Francois Paul De Grasse, commander of the French West Indies Fleet. Soon after the Secretary departed, De Grasse's flag-ship, Ville de Paris, fired a signal gun for departure and unfurled her fore-topsails---the voyage which was to take him to his place in history was under way. His fleet was made up of 36 sail-of-the-line, 3 frigates, 2 corvettes, 3 luggers, and 8 ships armed "in-flute".

* * * * *

Off-shore of Cape Charles, Virginia, Friday, March 16, 1781 dawned hazy, with fresh winds blowing. Admiral Marriot Arbuthnot's lookout frigate, IRIS, signaled at 6 A.M. "five strange ships in the NNE. large ships, about three miles distant, steering for the

Capes". At that time the British were about 42 miles NE BY E of Cape Henry, with the wind varying from West to WNW. Admiral Arbuthnot ordered the fleet to make ready for battle, and form a "line ahead".. The French, having seen the British, also started forming a "line ahead". After tacking and maneuvering for several hours, while the wind shifted to the Northeast and the seas built up, a little after 2 PM, the *ROBUST*, British ship-of-the-line, leading the Van of the fleet, began to engage the enemy.

Fighting was heavy for the next hour and a half, with the British claiming to have "broken the French line"; but, later admitting that the *ROBUST, PRUDENT, AND EUROPE* were so heavily damaged they could not keep up pursuit. At half past four a thick fog arose, effectively bringing the battle to a halt. Soon after, the British fleet headed for the Chesapeake, while the French withdrew. The French ships *CONQUERANT AND ARDENT* were heavily damaged in the encounter.

According to a French report, the French fleet actually arrived off Cape Charles on the 14th; but, because of heavy southwest winds, could not get into the bay, were driven northward, and tacked about for two whole days. Their report says the 16th dawned foggy. Adm. Destouches, aware he could not get into the bay and land his troops to support the assault on Portsmouth, was more concerned with protecting his force, rather than engaging in a sea battle: however, being aware of the necessity of defending his King's Honor, and not wanting the British to be able to boast that they had pursued him, resolved to attack their Van from the leeward position, so he could use his lower deck guns. The French ran to the southeast, all night, with shortened sail and all lights lit, but, in the morning the British were not to be seen.

Some time later, Lt. John Peebles, stationed in New York, wrote in his diary; "...various accounts of the late sea action off the Chesapeake accuse old Marriot of want of spirit and conduct, and some make reflections on the behaviour of the other ships." (based on report in Rivington's Royal Gazette 4/6/1781.)

* * * * *

About the 16th of March, General Lafayette, wanting to get a first hand view of the situation, arrived on the scene outside the British defenses at Portsmouth. ---But, news of the "stand-off" off the Capes meant the plan to attack Portsmouth and capture Arnold had to be postponed.

* * * * *

In New York, on the 24th, Gen. Clinton sent a letter to Gen. Phillips, who was on his way to Portsmouth; "...I believe Lord Cornwallis has finished his campaign...and, if reports are true, very handsomely, by taking all of Greene's cannon. ....if Lord Cornwallis does not want any cooperation to assist him, and you see no prospect of striking an important blow elsewhere, I shall probably request you and Arnold to return to me, with such troops as I have already named. ....all this will depend on the information I shall receive from you, and your opinion respecting the Post at Portsmouth...".[18]

Onboard the *ROYAL OAK*, in Lynnhaven Bay, Gen. William Phillips wrote Sir Henry Clinton, on March 26th, "The fleet, with my troops onboard, arrived off Chesapeake yesterday. We sailed into the Bay today to meet Adm. Arbuthnot. ...I hear the rebels are fortifying York and that there are heavy cannon there."[18]

With the arrival of Phillips' troops, there was now a combined force of over 3500 British at Portsmouth---too much for the force under Steuben to take on. He proposed taking 2000 picked militia and marching to join Gen. Greene near Halifax, N.C. This would give Greene greater strength than Cornwallis; and, hopefully, cause Phillips to leave Portsmouth and Virginia in order to aid Cornwallis. However, at the end of the month, Steuben wrote Greene, "...my desire to act under your orders and the disgust I have for my situation here (I am as tired of this state as they are of me.) are equal motive for my departure; however, I think it my duty to remain here." Steuben Papers, NYCPL

On the 29th, Gen. Phillips, mindful of Gen. Clinton's instructions about Adm. Arbuthnot, wrote a long letter to Clinton. In his opinion, the Admiral did not want to be connected with any enterprise in Virginia: Arbuthnot insisted his concern stopped at Lynnhaven Bay and the entrance to the Chesapeake. Arnold felt the Admiral would not give an opinion on any operation within the Bay area. Phillips spoke very highly of Arnold's cheerful intelligence and active zeal: "...I have found in him everything I could wish for in a Second." Clinton was also advised that Rebel forces around Portsmouth were about 3000, near Suffolk and the Northwest River bridge, under Gen. Muhlenberg. Gen. Weedon commanded 1600 at Williamsburg---all 4600 were Militia. ...He ended by saying he was returning enough transports to handle 3000 men.[16]

* * * * *

At headquarters, New Windsor, Conn, on March 31st, Gen. Washington wrote to Chevalier de La Luzerne, Comte Rochambeau, and Chevalier Destouches commiserating on the disappointing results of the Chesapeake venture, "...I think it may be fairly said that Great Britian owes the safety of her detachment under Arnold to the influence of the winds, and not to the superiority of her navy."[1]

With the departure of the French fleet, and postponement of action against Portsmouth, Governor Jefferson thought of the citizenry. He ordered Major Claiborne to have the impressed horses immediately returned to the owners, with compensation for loss of weight or injury. Lafayette was told a call had gone out for new militia drafts to replace those who had a long tour---the process should take about four weeks.

* * * *

April 2nd, Gen. Phillips, again, wrote Gen. Clinton: Cornwallis, although winning at Guilford Court House, suffered severely and had withdrawn down Cape Fear River to regroup. Lafayette's corps was still at Annapolis; and, if Gen. Clinton wanted Phillips to go after him---send more troops. It would not be possible

to send Gen. Arnold back to New York until after the
expedition up James River: "...he is of great utility
here---his knowledge of all water enterprises, with his
useful information of this country, render him necessary here, some time longer." Lord Cornwallis might be
able to get to the Chesapeake by June. Phillips wasn't
sure how he could help him in the meantime.

As for a post at Portsmouth---it would not do!
He suggested Norfolk and Tucker's Mill Point (present
day Portsmouth Naval Hospital,) which would protect
the Norfolk harbor, and if one were forced, a retreat
could be made to the other. However, the Chesapeake
must be secure, or once ships fled up the Elizabeth,
chased by a superior naval force, they must fall with
the post. Old Point Comfort might offer some possibili-
ties for escape routes, and would be explored.

"...As for our 'friends' in Norfolk and Princess
Anne Counties, they are timorous, cautious at best,
half friends, some, are concealed enemies. ...at present
they act sort of a saving game; but, are of no use to
us. On the whole, I lean in favor of a small post where
the army can assist the navy and the latter have a
chance of escaping a superior force. ...please do not
think I ask for more troops from a desire to parade
myself....I assure you I do not. If you mean only little
enterprises in this vicinity, we are enough. ...if you
wish a strong and serious cooperation with Lord Cornwallis, and a positive blow struck in the Chesapeake,
....it can't be done with the force I now have."[11]

* * * * *

At Boston, on April 4th, Gen. Benjamin Lincoln,
late British captive at Charleston, received a letter
from his Commander, Gen. Washington: "...every day
convinces me the enemy are determined to send their
force against the southern states. We must support
those states powerfully from here or they will be lost.

I am sure the detachment under Phillips is intended
for Cornwallis. Should they join forces, Greene's
present force will not enable him to give any effectual
opposition. ...You well know that collecting militia depends entirely on prospects of the day. If favorable,
they throng to you; if not, they will not move. "[1]

On the 6th, Washington wrote Lafayette; "..your corps should proceed immediately to join the Southern Army. ...inform Gen. Greene you are on your way to join him and take his directions as to your route."[1]

At the same time, Gen. William Heath advised Washington that an informant had brought news of a British plot to take or assassinate Washington, the Governor of New Jersey, and the Governor of New York. Washington replied, "...guarding against assassination, (which I neither expect nor dread) is impossible; but, I have not been without apprehension of the other---not from the enemy, but, the tories, who might, in the night, carry me off in my own boat."[1]

* * * * *

In London, April 7th, former Virginia Governor Dunmore "called out" all Virginia Loyalists: "...Having received His Majesty's command to return to Virginia, I am directed to inform you, you are expected to go with me or relinquish allowances paid you. ...to enable you to fit out for this voyage, you will be given a year's allowance, and free passage to Virginia."[11]

* * * * *

From Portsmouth, Gen. Phillips wrote Cornwallis, "...I shall be ready to move on the 12th--with 2000 effective men....the plan will be to break communication from Virginia to North Carolina. ...The time I shall be able to remain depends on Lafayette. If he moves from Annapolis with his 1800 Continental troops and militia he can gather, it will force me to return to guard this place. ...in doing so, I shall destroy every public store, all vessels, boats, and mills so as to render the country as much incapable of acting as possible."[11]

At Wilmington, N.C., Cornwallis wrote Gen. Clinton, on April 10th; "...I am impatiently looking for the expected reinforcements from Europe, part of which are indispensably necessary for me to act offensively. ...I am very anxious to receive Your Excellency's orders, being totally in the dark as to the intended summer operations. I cannot help expressing my wishes that the Chesapeake may become the seat of the war, even (if necessary) at the expense of abandoning New York. Until Virginia is subdued, our hold on the Carolinas must be difficult, if not precarious."[16]

Cornwallis also wrote Phillips, at Portsmouth, "now, my friend, what is our plan? ...I am tired of marching about the country seeking adventure. If we mean offensive war in America, we must abandon New York and bring our whole force into Virginia: we then have a stake to fight for and a successful battle may give us America. But, if our plan is defensive, mixed with desultory expeditions, let us quit the Carolinas, which cannot be held defensively, while Virginia can be so easily armed against, and stick to our salt pork and New York, sending, now and then, a detachment to steal tobacco. I can come to you by land; but, whether, after we join, we shall have sufficient force for a war of conquest, I think very doubtful. ..."[17]

* * * * *

All was not well in the American camp: earlier in April, from Virginia, Gen. Muhlenberg advised Gen. Steuben; "...the militia who have served their three months have partly discharged themselves, compelling me to discharge the rest. ...100 deserted from my camp in one night." (Steuben papers, New York)

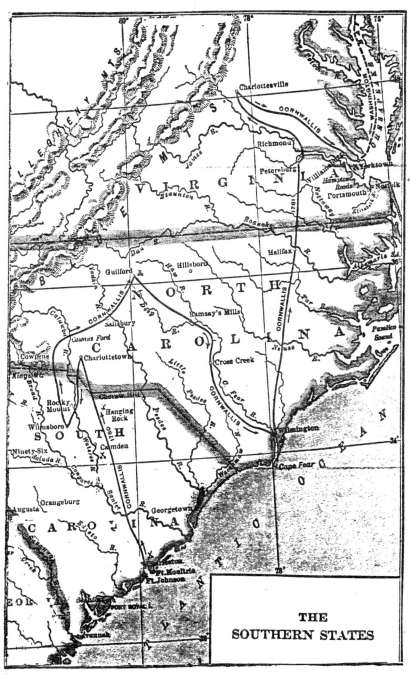

Route of Cornwallis' army from Charleston
to Yorktown---and capitulation

CHAPTER FOUR
At the end of our tether!

At Philadelphia, on April 10th, while waiting to depart for France, Col. John Laurens received one of the most candid letters George Washington ever wrote: "...day does not follow night more certainly, than it brings with it some additional proof of the impracticability of carrying on the war without the aids you are directed to solicit. As an honest and candid man...whose all depends on the final and happy termination of the present contest, I assure you this....without a foreign loan, our present force, which is but the remnant of an army, cannot be kept together through this campaign. ...if France delays a timely and powerful aid in this critical posture of our affairs, it will avail us nothing should she attempt it hereafter: we are, at this hour, suspended in the balle; not from choice, but from hard and absolute necessity....we cannot transport the provisions from the states, where they are, to the army, where it is, because we cannot pay the teamsters, who will no longer work for certificates. ...our troops are approaching fast to nakedness...our hospitals are without medicine. ...in a word, *We are at the end of our tether!*"[1]

On April 11th, Washington wrote Lafayette, "...If I had any prospect of an operation against New York, such as you spoke of, I would consider your detachment essential to the undertaking; but, I can assure you, without entering into the many reasons (which I cannot commit to paper), I have not, at present, any idea of being able to effect such a maneuver."[1]

* * * * *

On the other side, at New York, a frustrated Gen. Clinton, wrote Gen. Phillips chiding him for getting his priorities mixed and fortifying Portsmouth rather than acting in support of Lord Cornwallis, as Arnold had also been instructed. In addition, Arnold had advised Portsmouth was in good preparedness and defendable by his forces---now Phillips, with 2000 more troops, was questioning its state of readiness and suitability. He had never expected Portsmouth to be a major post..."God forbid that I should think of burying the elite of my army in Nansemond and Princess Anne. If you and Arnold have good reason to condemn it, leave it! All I want is a station that can protect the King's ships, garrisoned by 500-600 men."[11]

On April 15th, before receiving the above, Phillips again wrote Gen. Clinton, "...I am brought to declare Portsmouth a bad Post: its locality not calculated for defense, collateral points necessary to be taken are so many that a great number of troops would be required. ...in all my letters, I have taken the liberty to remark that I thought this post could not be secured without a great number of troops. ...but, taking into consideration the sort of enemy we face on the move I am about to make, the post will be secure with the troops I shall leave in it."[11]

On April 18th, once again bypassing his Commander, Cornwallis wrote his friend at court Lord Germain, "...the principle reason for under-taking the winter campaign were, the difficulty of a defensive war in South Carolina, and hopes that our friends in North Carolina, said to be numerous, would make good their promises of taking an active part with us. ...experience has shown their numbers not as great as represented and their friendship passive.
Therefore, if it is in the interest of Great Britain to maintain what she already possesses, and to press the war in the southern provinces, I take the liberty of giving my opinion that a serious attempt on Virginia would be the most solid plan. The great reinforcements sent by Virginia to Greene. while Arnold was in the Chesapeake, are convincing proof that small expeditions do not frighten that powerful province."[11] Obviously, Cornwallis is promoting a separate command for the southern colonies with himself as commander---reporting directly to London.

Col. John Graves Simcoe diaried for April 18th, "having completed the works at Portsmouth, we embarked and dropped down to Hampton Roads. Gen. Phillips informed us the expedition was to attack a body of the enemy stationed at Williamsburg."

In his diary for the day, Dr. Robert Honeyman noted, "the British landed at Burwell's Bay and marched to Williamsburg with 300 men. Col. Innes, who commanded the Virginia militia, withdrew to a point nearer to Richmond. Col. Simcoe led a party of British cavalry to Yorktown where they spiked the guns."

* * * * *

On April 21st, after reviewing his intelligence on all of the latest British troop movements, Washington penned another note to Lafayette, "...from the present aspect of things, it is most probable the weight of the war, this campaign, will be in the southern states, and it will become my duty to go there in person; where I shall have the pleasure of seeing you again. ..."[1]

At last, Washington is realizing that his hopes for a siege of New York will not come to fruition: his French allies are not in favor of a naval confrontation at New York; without which, a siege will not succeed. But! something is afoot in Virginia and the Chesapeake, and he will go there.

* * * * *

While Gen. Phillips was moving his troops up the James River towards Richmond and Petersburg, Gen. Cornwallis, in Wilmington, wrote Minister Germain, on April 23rd, "I have resolved to take advantage of Greene's leaving the back of Virginia open and march there immediately to make a junction with Phillips." [1]

That same day, Cornwallis also wrote his Commander, Gen. Clinton, "...neither my cavalry nor infantry are ready to move, the former want for everything, the latter, every necessity but shoes. ...I must, however, begin our march tomorrow. It is very hard for me to decide on measures so important without an opportunity of procuring your Excellency's direction, or approval; but, the delay and difficulty in conveying letters, and impossibility of awaiting answers, render it necessary. ...As I find there is no prospect of speedy reinforcements from Europe, and the return of Greene to North Carolina...would put a junction with Phillips out of my power, I have resolved to march immediately for Virginia, to attempt that junction."[1]

Phillips' army entered Petersburg on the 25th, and, with it as a base, spent the next two weeks rampaging around the countryside, to Manchester, Chesterfield Courthouse, Osbornes, Hood's Point, seizing and burning hogsheads of tobacco, supplies and ships.

On the 26th, Cornwallis wrote Phillips telling of a diversionary move towards Hillsborough to try to draw Greene back into North Carolina. "If that should not succeed, I shall be much tempted to join you. This will be exceedingly hazardous and many unforeseen difficulties may render it totally impractical. ...you must not take any steps to expose your army to the dangers of ruin. ...we will march to the lowest ford of the Roanoke....send every possible intelligence...make every movement in your power to facilitate our junction, which must be near Petersburg."[1]

* * * * *

Not having received any of the letters Cornwallis wrote in February, March, or April, Gen. Clinton wrote Phillips on April 30th; "I cannot tell from Lord Cornwallis' letters if he plans further operations in the Carolinas, what they may be, or how far you can operate in his favor. My private opinion is that he has no offensive objective in view."[1] Clinton then lists the troops with Cornwallis and Phillips and asks how he could possibly want more! He suggests that if they cannot agree on an action, Phillips and Arnold should make a move, up Chesapeake Bay, against Philadelphia. If that failed, they could return to Portsmouth or cross the Delaware---where Clinton would join them. "...unless things take a more favorable turn, I should imagine His Lordship will not leave Carolina."[1] [Clinton, at that writing, had no idea that Gen.

Cornwallis was five days on the road to a junction with Phillips, near Halifax, N.C., which probably took place before Phillips got this letter.]

Clinton continued, "...our Admiral has grown, if possible, more impractical than ever: he swears to me he knows nothing of his recall---to others, he says he is going home immediately. If the next packet boat does not satisfy me in this particular, I shall probably retire and leave him to Lord Cornwallis management."[18]

The same day, Clinton, wrote another letter to Cornwallis, "...as it is probable your Lordship's presence in Carolina cannot be soon ended, I hope you will communicate to Gen. Phillips your plan for future operations in that quarter: also, your opinion as to how the Chesapeake Army can best help you. Phillips has 3500 men under him, and I shall send him 1700 more whenever the Admiral is ready. Phillips is instructed to act in Your Lordship's favor, to the best of his judgement, until he receives your orders. ...I was in hopes your successes in N. Carolina would have been such that I might avail myself of a large part of Your Lordship's army, the whole Chesapeake Corps, and the entire reenforcement from Europe---for a campaign to the Northward of Carolina. I must defer fixing on that plan, until I am acquainted with the success of Your Lordship's operation. ..."[18]

May 6th, while onboard the *MESSA*, off Burwells Bay, (on the James River, near Smithfield) Gen. Phillips wrote Cornwallis, "...I received your letter of the 26th an hour ago. ...Lafayette is up near the James with about 1500 men...I can easily keep his corps in subjection. ...You should have no difficulty making a junction with me. ...I will do everything possible to contact Your Lordship from Petersburg. ...I was returning to Portsmouth after a successful expedition up the James, having destroyed all the State's armed vessels, merchant ships, etc., plus a large quantity of wheat flour in kegs and 6000 hogsheads of tobacco. I am now sailing back up river and should reach Petersburg tomorrow. ...it will give me great satisfaction if my corps can be of service to Your Lordship's operations.

Had you been positive of coming to the Roanoke River, I would have made a forced march to meet you."[16]

* * * * *

Admiral DeGrasse's French fleet, 20 ships-of-the-line, arrived at Martinique, French West Indies, April 29th. Finding an 18 ship British fleet blockading the port, De Grasse challenged them to an action---it ended with the British sailing for Port Royal.

In Newport, Rhode Island, on May 6th, there was great rejoicing over the arrival of the French Frigate *CONCORDE* bringing Gen. Rochambeau's son, and Admiral De Barras, new commander of the French fleet at Newport. Rejoicing subsided when it was learned the French King had not sent more troops---but, he had authorized a six million Franc loan to the Americans.

On May 7th, at Richmond, the Virginia General Assembly, hearing of the reappearance of Phillips Army near Hoods, RESOLVED: "...because of the approach of an hostile army, from whose operations the deliberations of this Assembly may be greatly interrupted, impeded, or totally prevented: that this house be adjourned until Thursday the 24th, then to meet in the town of Charlottesville, County of Albemarle."[51]

* * * * *

Writing from Petersburg, on May 12th, Gen. Benedict Arnold advised Gen. Cornwallis, "...Phillips is here in force to cooperate with Your Lordship's wishes. ...we suppose Your Lordship to be either at Halifax or on this side of the Roanoke. Lafayette is on the opposite side of the Appomattox, and Wayne is on his way to Richmond with the Pennsylvania Line. ...a reenforcement was requested from N.Y. by Gen. Phillips and it was to sail for Portsmouth on the 6th."[16]

Just prior to his return to Petersburg, Gen. Phillips was taken violently ill:---he died on May 13th, before joining up with Cornwallis. He was buried at Blanford Church, Petersburg.

On the 17th, Cornwallis wrote Arnold, "...I have just received yours of last night---the death of my dear friend Phillips gives me much grief. ...my reason for ordering you to march to the Nottaway was to prevent the Marquis (Lafayette) from bringing you to action before I could join you.---that consideration ceases. I am so unacquainted with the Post at Portsmouth and the situation of your ships, I cannot give immediate orders. ...leave your corps where this finds you; and bring your cavalry to meet me at Butler's Bridge early tomorrow morning. "[16]

From the Virginia-Carolina border, Earl Cornwallis wrote Gen. Clinton, "...Gen. Arnold opines that Portsmouth, with its present garrison, is secure against an attack. I wish to avoid an early movement to that place without absolute necessity. I have assured the Commander there that I will do everything to relieve him in the event of a French attack.

By your recent letters, I find you think that if an offensive army could be spared, it would not be wise to employ it in this province. As the security of South Carolina and reduction of North Carolina, seemed to be expected of me, in this country and in England, I felt called on to point out that, in my opinion, until Virginia was subjugated, we could not reduce North Carolina, nor have any hold on its back country... .Having replaced Gen. Phillips, I felt called on, by you, to give my opinion on the attempt on Philadelphia. ....I would cautiously engage in measures depending materially for success on assistance from the country. ...and, I think the attempt on Philadelphia would do more harm than good to the cause of Britain."[18]

* * * * *

In Paris, France, on May 14th, Foreign Minister Vergennes wrote Chevalier de Luzerne, French Consul at Philadelphia, "...you may confide to Gen. Washington that de Grasse has express orders, after providing for the safety of our Islands, to detach or take the greater part of his fleet to ...North America, and lend themselves to all operations judged practicable for as long as the season will permit remaining there. If the Spanish are not in need of reinforcements from our troops, all of them will join you..."[11]

On May 20th, another member of Washington's staff appeared at Weathersfield, Conn: Gen. Henry Knox, Commander of American artillery, wrote his brother, William, "...I am here, my dear brother, having arrived last evening with General Washington and Gen Duportail to meet with Gen. Rochambeau and Admiral Barras on matters of real consequence." At this conference, Rochambeau posed the question, "...in the event of a French naval reenforcement from the West Indies, what operations shall be undertaken by the combined allied forces." Washington answered, "...the combined force may either proceed in operations against New York, or be directed against the enemy in some other quarter, as circumstances dictate. ..."[1]

May 23rd Washington wrote French Ambassador Luzerne, at Philadelphia, "..it is not for me to know in what manner the French fleet is to be employed in the West Indies...or when it may be expected on this coast; but, that appearance is so important to any offensive operation, I hope I will be excused for trying to engage your good offices in facilitating an event on which so much depends. ...I assure you that Gen. Rochambeau's opinion and wishes concur with mine, and it is at his instance, primarily, I make this request. Count de Rochambeau and Chevalier Chastellux agree perfectly in sentiment with me that, while affairs remain as they are now , the West Indies Fleet should run immediately to Sandy Hook (N.J.) where it would be met with further directions, and where, most likely, it will either shut in or cut off Admiral Arbuthnot, and also be joined by Count de Barras. An early communication from Admiral De Grasse would lead to our preparatory measures, and facilitate the operation in hand--or any other which may be thought advisable."[1]

* * * * *

Lafayette, in Virginia, wrote Washington on May 24th, "...I am caught between two problems: If I fight a battle, I will be cut to pieces, the militia dispersed, and our arms lost. If I decline to fight, the people of the country will think themselves given up. Therefore,

I am determined to skirmish, but not to engage too far, and take particular care against their excellent body of horse, which the militia fear as they would some wild beasts. ....were I in anyway equal to the enemy, I would be very happy in my present command; but, I am not even strong enough to be beaten. Government here has no energy, and laws no force."[1]

* * * * *

From Berkley Plantation, on the James, Cornwallis wrote Gen. Clinton; "May 26, ...the reinforcements arrived in James River and I have sent Gen. Leslie to Portsmouth with the 17th Regiment and the two battalions of Anspach, keeping the 43rd. I shall proceed to dislodge Lafayette from Richmond, destroy any magazines in the vicinity, then move down the peninsula to Williamsburg....keeping myself unengaged until I hear from you on plans for the campaign. ...I hope I shall have an opportunity to receive better information than hitherto relative to a proper harbor and a safe place of arms. At present, I am inclined to think well of York. The objections to Portsmouth are, it cannot be made strong without an army to defend it, it is remarkably unhealthy, and can give no protection to a ship-of-the-line."

"...One maxim appears to me as absolutely necessary for the safe and honorable conduct of the war: it is, that we should be in respectable force. By vigorous exertions of the present governors of Virginia, large bodies of men are soon collected; and, I have too often observed that when a storm threatens, our friends disappear. ...I take the liberty of repeating--- if an offensive war is intended, Virginia appears to me the only province in which it can be carried on...but, to reduce the province and keep possession of the countryside, a considerable army would be needed ."[11]

In the same letter, Cornwallis also said, "...I have consented to General Arnold's request to return to New York; he feels that Your Excellency wishes him to attend you there, and, his present indisposition makes him unequal to the fatigue of this service. He will report to you the horrid enormities committed by our privateers in Chesapeake Bay. It is my earnest wish that some remedy be found for this evil...so very prejudicial to His Majesty's service."[18]

The "horrid enormities" Cornwallis referred to was the pillaging of the countryside farms and people by the crews of the so-called British privateers who had entered the Bay. Their commissions limited them to capturing sailing vessels, but, finding none, they sought booty ashore---taking from rebel and Loyalist!

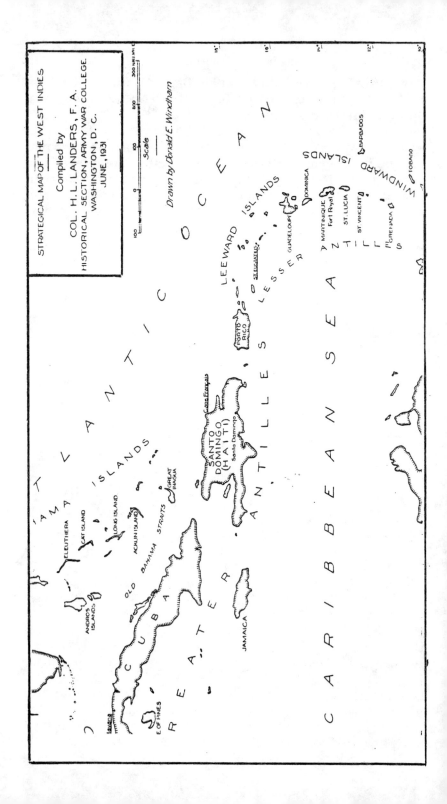

STRATEGICAL MAP OF THE WEST INDIES

Compiled by
COL. H. L. LANDERS, F. A.
HISTORICAL SECTION, ARMY WAR COLLEGE,
WASHINGTON, D. C.
JUNE, 1931

Scale

Drawn by Donald E. Windham

ATLANTIC OCEAN

BAHAMA ISLANDS

ELEUTHERA

CAT ISLAND

LONG ISLAND

ACKLIN ISLAND

GREAT INAGUA

OLD BAHAMA STRAITS

ANDROS ISLANDS

CUBA

I. OF PINES

GREATER ANTILLES

JAMAICA

SANTO DOMINGO (HAITI)

Santo Domingo

Cape François

PORTO RICO

LEEWARD ISLANDS

ST. KITTS

GUADELOUPE

LESSER

DOMINICA

MARTINIQUE
Fort Royal

ST. LUCIA

ST. VINCENT

GRENADA

BARBADOS

WINDWARD ISLANDS

TOBAGO

CARIBBEAN SEA

CHAPTER FIVE

RESOLVED: Call out the militia.

From Newport, on May 28th, Gen. Rochambeau wrote Admiral DeGrasse, in the West Indies, "...The enemy is making most vigorous efforts in Virginia. Cornwallis marched from Wilmington to join Phillips at the Roanoke River. Their army of 6000 marched to Portsmouth; from there they ravage all the rivers of Virginia. Washington assures me he has no more than 8500 regulars and 3000 militia for carrying on a campaign against New York. ...that is the state of affairs and the grave crisis in which America, and especially the southern states, finds herself at this time. The arrival of Comte de Grasse would save this situation. All the means at our hands are not enough without his joint action and the sea superiority at his command. "

...two points where an offensive may be made against the enemy: Chesapeake Bay and New York. Southwesterly winds and the state of distress in Virginia will probably make you prefer the Chesapeake. It is there we think you may render the greatest service. ...you would need only two days from there to New York. In any case, it is essential you send a frigate, well in advance, to inform Barras and Washington where you are to come. ....It is needless to write of the important service you can render if you bring a body of troops with your ships."[14]

The same day, Virginia's Governor Jefferson wrote his friend George Washington, "I am sure you have heard...of the junction of Lord Cornwallis with the forces under Arnold at Petersburg. ...From the best intelligence I have, the whole force of the enemy within this state is about seven thousand men. ...If it is possible for this situation to justify your lending us your personal aid, it is evident from the voice of the people that the presence of their beloved countryman....would restore full confidence of salvation... ."[5]

*　*　*　*　*

May 29th, Sir Henry Clinton, in New York, wrote Earl Cornwallis, in Virginia, telling him his operations in Virginia would only be secure as long as the British fleet was in control of the Chesapeake: "...in which case, I hope Your Lordship will be able to place your army in a secure situation during such a temporary inconvenience---for should it become permanent, I need not say what our prospects in this country are likely to be. I have urgently requested Admiral Arbuthnot's attention to the Chesapeake....and repeatedly told him that, should the enemy possess it, even for 48 hours, Your Lordship's operation would be exposed to eminent danger. Gen. Robertson has also tried to impress him....I cannot be sure he will, as I do, consider the Chesapeake the first object. At present he seems inclined to take his fleet to open the post at Rhode Island.."[11] This view differed from the one Clinton expressed to Gen. Phillips earlier.

*　*　*　*　*

In Charlottesville, Virginia, on May 29th, the Virginia House of Delegates, RESOLVED: ...because of a powerful army of the enemy inflicting miseries and calamities of war on our friends and fellow citizens in the lower counties....the Governor is desired to immediately, and with all possible expedition, order into service such a number of militia as will enable the commander of the army to oppose the enemy with effect....and that he is urged to tell Major General Marquis de Lafayette, that, under present circumstances , this state cannot consent to public arms being sent out of state."[31] While this Resolution was heroic in intentions, it had little effect as almost all of Virginia's men were already under arms in eastern Virginia or had been sent to other states to assist them.

On the 31st, Washington wrote Lafayette of a conference at Weathersfield, and said, "...upon a full consideration of our affairs, from every point of view, an attempt upon New York, with its present garrison estimated reduced to about 4500 men, was deemed preferable to a southern operation as we do not have command of the off-shore waters. ...We have rumors, though I cannot say they are well founded, that the enemy are about to quit New York altogether. ...Should they do this, we must follow them as they can have no other view than endeavoring to seize and secure the southern states: if not to hold them firmly, to make them means of an advantageous negotiation of peace."[1]

* * * * *

Clinton wrote Cornwallis, on June 1st, "...I have just received the Admiral's answer to my letter and am assured from it he will do everything in his power to guard the Chesapeake. ...respecting my opinion of stations on James and York rivers; I refer Your Lordship to my instructions to Generals Phillips and Arnold...to which I referred you in my last dispatch. I shall, of course, approve any alterations you think proper to make in those stations. ...detachments I have made from this army to the Chesapeake, since Gen. Leslie's October expedition, amount to 7,724 effectives. At the time Your Lordship made the junction with Gen. Phillips, there were 5,304 in his command---a force, I should hope to be sufficient to carry on any operation in any of the southern colonies. ..."[11]

At Portsmouth, Gen. Leslie wrote Cornwallis, on June 3rd, "...Public and private ships have been plundering up the Bay and on the Eastern Shore: a stop must be put to it as our Loyalist friends complain bitterly! If Your Lordship would ask Capt. Hammond, of the *RICHMOND*, to forbid all ships from going up the rivers or Bay: ...there are no prizes now on the water and they, of course, should not go ashore."[11]

* * * * *

From Whitehall, England, June 4th, Lord Germain wrote to Cornwallis: "...the King has commanded me to signify to Your Lordship His Majesty's Royal approbation of your able conduct, unremitting exertions, and ardent zeal for his service. ...I was much alarmed to read Sir Henry Clinton's to General Phillips, instructing him to return to New York with the greatest part of his force, if he did not receive orders from you.

...your victory at Guiliford will have opened the country more and afforded you an opportunity to take him and his force under your command and employ it as a joint army until the southern provinces are reduced. ...it is the King's firm purpose to recover those provinces in preference to all others, and to push the war from south to north, securing what is conquered as we go on. ...I have signified His Majesty's pleasure to Sir Henry Clinton, to that effect."[1]

Two days later, Lord Germain wrote Gen. Clinton; "...I am well pleased to find Lord Cornwallis opinion coincides with mine——of the greatest importance of pushing the war in Virginia, with all the force that can be spared, until that province is reduced. ..."[1]

Germain's two letters highlight the problem Gen. Clinton faced in running a campaign in America: 1. A Second in Command who had his own opinion about where and how to wage the campaign, and had no compunctions about bypassing his Commander and going to the Secretary for North American Affairs with his own ideas. 2. A Secretary who, though 3000 miles away, would allow a Second to do this, and favor those ideas over those of the Commander in Chief.

Clinton appears unable/unwilling to give a "flat-out" order/directive to Cornwallis, Phillips, Leslie, or Arnold: he always qualified them with something like, "if Your/His Lordship approves, if not, do what you/he desire(s)." Cornwallis usually followed that option. Whether Clinton did this in deference to London and Nobility, or because he felt he should give latitude to his Field Commanders when in distant fields and facing poor communications, is a hard question to answer. Whichever, the lack of positive direction certainly worked against him and the interest of Great Britian.

On June 8th, Gen. Clinton dispatched an order to the commanding officer at Portsmouth; "...should any reinforcements arrive in the Chesapeake from Europe, I request that they not be disembarked, but proceed to join me here in New York."[1]

* * * * *

In Staunton, Virginia, on Tuesday, June 10, the General Assembly of Virginia elected Thomas Nelson Jr. to be Governor and Chief Magistrate of the Commonwealth. Nelson had been serving as a Militia General.[14]

From Newport, Rhode Island, June 11th, French General Rochambeau wrote French Admiral de Grasse; "...I must not conceal from you, Monsieur, the Americans are at the end of their resources. Washington will not have half of the troops he is reckoned to have, and I believe, though he is silent on it, that at present he does not have 6000 men, and that M. de Lafayette does not have 1000 regulars with militia to defend Virginia. ...it is therefore of the utmost importance that you bring in your ships the largest number of soldiers possible, 4000 or 5000 will be none too many. ...I am certain you will give us maritime superiority, but I cannot tell you too often to bring soldiers and money."---A later letter added, "...this country is in extremity; all its resources have failed at once. Continental paper has become worthless."[15]

On June 13th, Washington again wrote Rochambeau about what De Grasse should do; "...Your Excellency will please recollect that New York was looked upon by us as the only practicable objective under present circumstances; but, should we be able to secure a naval superiority, we might find others more practicable and equally advisable. Instead of advising the Admiral to run immediately into the Chesapeake, will it not be better to leave him to judge from the information he may, from time to time, receive of the situation of the enemy's fleet upon this coast?"[16]

* * * * *

The same day, Gen. Clinton wrote Gen. Cornwallis; "...I beg leave to recommend to you, as soon as you have finished the active operations you are now engaged in, to take a defensive station in any healthy situation you choose, be it Williamsburg or Yorktown, and, in that case, I wish that after reserving to yourself such troops as you may judge necessary for an ample defensive and desultory move-

ment....the following corps may be sent to me, as you
can spare them...two battalions of light infantry, the
43rd, the 76th or 80th, two battalions of Anspach,
Queens Rangers, cavalry and infantry...and such a
proportion of artillery as can be spared."[11] He went
on to discuss their difference of opinion as to whether
a move into Pennsylvania is wise, Clinton saying it is,
and if he continues in command---it will be tried!

From London, on June 22nd, Phillip Stephens,
Secretary of the Navy, wrote Admiral Graves, in New
York, "...His Majesty commands me to acquaint you that
Rear Admiral Digby is appointed to command His
Majesty's ships employed in North America. ...Their
Lordships advise me to inform you that, as the squad-
ron in Jamaica has been much diminished by the late
hurricane, you will receive orders to proceed in the
LONDON to reinforce that squadron."[9]

This message, its date of origin, and receipt by
Graves, Sept. 12, points out that events generally
moved more rapidly than communications! The problem
was especially acute for the British. The Lords of the
Admiralty never planned for Admiral Graves to take
command of the North Atlantic Squadron. He was being
advised that Adm. Digby would get that command and
Graves was being sent to the West Indies.

This notification was written 12 days before
Graves was advised by his commanding officer, Admiral
Arbuthnot, [July 4th] that he was returning to Eng-
land early (prior to Digby's arrival) and Graves, was
being given interim command of the North American
Squadron. Graves would not receive this letter of
reassignment until he returned to New York [approx.
Sept 12th]---after his ill-fated battle with the French
Fleet off the Capes of Virginia, Sept. 5th.

* * * * *

At Barbados, British West Indies; June 24th,
Adm. Samuel Hood wrote Lord Jackson, in London, "It
is impossible, from the unsteadiness of the Commander-
in-Chief [Adm. Rodney] to know what he means, three
days together; first he says physical problems prevent

his remaining here, and he will leave the command to
me, next, he says he has no thought of going home."[1]
"The French now have twenty eight two-decked ships.
at Fort Royal Bay, ...I imagine they will. move to St.
Domingo by the end of next month, if not sooner, take
all the trade from these islands, and proceed to
Europe in great force. Probably, a part will separate
off Bermuda and go to Rhode Island."[1]

"..accounts from New York of the [March] skirmish
off the Virginia coast are much against the Naval Commander-in-Chief." He then discusses the raid on St.
Eustatius..."the treasures .... were so bewitching as
not to be withstood by flesh and blood. ...the Admiral
and General Vaughan have a great deal to answer for,
which I told them long ago. ...they are now in a
squeeze as many of their actions will not well bear the
daylight. ...the Commanders could not bear the thought
of leaving the money behind, and not withstanding
their loud talk of disregard of money, they will find
it difficult to convince the world that they have not
proved themselves wicked in their plundering."[1]

Adm. Hood correctly predicted that the St.
Eustatius raid would have ramifications far beyond the
West Indies; although he could not have foreseen the
most important one: As Fleet Admiral, Rodney was
entitled to a percentage of the value of all ships and
cargo taken in the raid; he decided to return to
England with the convoy rather than take his entire
fleet to New York. Had Rodney gone to New York, he
would have commanded the British fleet at the Battle
off the Capes of Virginia. Considered a better tactician
than Graves, and more aggressive, the outcome of the
battle would have, undoubtedly, been different.

In New York, Lt. John Peebles' diaried on June
27th, "...we hear by the Pacquet boat that old Marriot
is recalled and Admiral Digby will take command." This
time, news came before the event. New York knew of
Digby's coming before his arrival; but Adm. Arbuthnot,
not waiting to be relieved, made an early departure
and turned interim command over to Admiral Graves."[1]

* * * * *

On June 27th, in Virginia, Militia Gen. Weedon wrote Lafayette, "...I have always thought the British would finally settle in Williamsburg. The advantages of that place, the countryside from there to Hampton--- covered by a few redoubts, the advantage of Navigation on both York and James Rivers: if we can prevent a chain from Queens Creek on York to College Creek on James, I think his Lordship will find us trouble-- some. While I don't think the time is right for any serious action, close skirmishing might be proper...to frustrate those mighty champions, and circumscribe their depredations--- *A victory to this country!*"[aa]

From Smithfield, on James River, Col. Josiah Parker wrote Governor Thomas Nelson "...I am told the British routed Gen. Gregory's Carolina militia from Northwest Bridge yesterday. Princess Anne and Norfolk counties, and all of Nansemond below Suffolk have virtually surrendered to the enemy and are now very dangerous to us. Unless something is done with the people below Suffolk, my position will be very disagreeable. They are worse than the enemy!"[bb]

* * * * *

In New York, on the 27th, Still thinking of Northern operations having a priority over those in Virginia and the Chesapeake, Gen. Clinton wrote Gen. Leslie, at Portsmouth, "...I have determined on an expedition against Philadelphia to endeavor to seize public stores collected there....If it can be done without destroying the town. I have appointed Lt. Gen. Robertson for that service. ..."[cc]

Paused at Williamsburg, Cornwallis wrote Leslie, "orders from New York make it necessary for me to give up all thought of a post on this side of James River: stop all of the detachments ordered up, except that part of the 80th. ....I am very unwilling to forego fixing a place for arms at York, if it is possible to effect it consistent with the arrangement of the force in this country. Tomorrow, I shall go to York to examine that place before I make my final resolution.

As the war in Virginia is to be only defensive, except some desultory expeditions, all ideas in favor of the Carolinas must cease; consequently, the war in South Carolina will be kept up by the enemy as long as we attempt to hold any part of the province. In that case, I think either you or I should go there: perhaps you may go..., then I will relieve you. ..."¹⁸

At the same time, Cornwallis wrote his Commander-in-Chief, Gen. Clinton, on the 30th, "...on my arrival here, I was honored with Your Excellency's dispatches of the 11th and 15th; I find you think if an offensive army could be spared, it would not be advisable to employ it in this province. ...as the security of South Carolina, if not the reduction of North Carolina, seemed to be generally expected of me, in this country and in England, I thought myself called upon, after the experiment I made had failed, to point out the only mode, in my opinion, of effecting it, and to declare that until Virginia was to a degree subjected, we could not reduce North Carolina, or have any hold on the back country of South Carolina."

"Having replaced Gen Phillips, I felt called upon, by you, for my opinion of an attempt on Philadelphia. Having experienced much disappointment with loyalists, I said I would cautiously engage in measures materially depending for their success on assistance from them, and I thought the attempt on Philadelphia would do much harm to the cause of Britian."

On viewing York, I was of opinion that it far exceeds our power, consistent with your plans, to make safe defensive posts there and at Gloucester, both would be necessary for protection of shipping. As soon as I cross the James and can load a convoy with troops, they shall be dispatched to you: others will follow as fast as you send transports to carry them. When I see Portsmouth, I shall give my opinion of the troops necessary for its defense, or any other posts thought proper. As there is little chance of establishing a post capable of giving effective protection to ships of war, I ask Your Excellency if it is worthwhile to hold a sickly defensive post in this Bay, which will always be exposed to a sudden French attack." ¹⁹

60

"As I do not think it possible to render any service in a defensive situation here, I am willing to return to Charleston, if you approve."[18]

Cornwallis, who previously said that until Virginia was subdued, the South could not be taken and controlled, is now saying the Chesapeake would always be vulnerable, good for defensive posts only, and offering to go back to Charleston. On the other hand, Clinton, who once said posts on the Chesapeake should be for defense and "desultory raids", is now saying it should be taken and never left! This argument continued after the war and was carried on in testimonials and publications.

The first of July, Clinton dispatched to Gen. Leslie, in Portsmouth, "...Whenever the troops Lord Cornwallis shall have embarked under your orders are ready to sail, it is the Admiral's and my wish that the courier frigate should return to us: forty-eight hours after she leaves the Chesapeake, you will put to sea and proceed to Delaware Bay where you will hover out of sight until joined by the Admiral...."[19]

In New York harbor, July 4th, Adm. Marriot Arbuthnot wrote his second in command, Adm. Thomas Graves, "...Mr. Stephens, Admiralty Secretary, in a letter of 3rd May signified approval by the Lords Commissioners of my desire to return home after resigning command of His Majesty's ships in North America to any senior officer on the spot. I enclose an extract of that letter, also a list and disposition of the squadron, and a schedule of papers and intelligence necessary for your guidance in conducting the command. I hereby resign command of the squadron into your hands, wishing you all imaginable success and happiness...."[20] Ships of the squadron were; *EUROPE - 74, RUSSELL-74, ROBUST-74, DEFIANCE-64, ADAMANT-50,* five 44s, seven 32s, four 28s, etc.[21]

* * * * *

In Virginia, Lafayette wrote Governor Nelson, "...there is no keeping the militia in the field: many are deserting, but it is next to impossible to take them in their flight through the woods. They say they were only engaged for six months and harvest time calls them home. You might as well try to stop the flood tide as to stop militia whose time has run out...."[55]

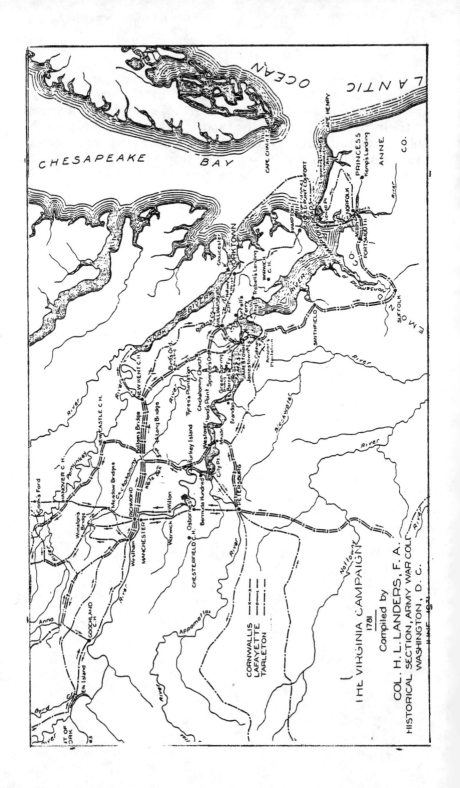

THE VIRGINIA CAMPAIGN
1781

Compiled by
COL. H. L. LANDERS, F. A.
HISTORICAL SECTION, ARMY WAR COLLEGE
WASHINGTON, D. C.
JUNE 1931

CORNWALLIS ——x——x——
LAFAYETTE ——o——o——
TARLETON — — — —

CHAPTER SIX

Forget Portsmouth--take York.

In the French West Indies, on July 8th, Admiral de Grasse received the courier frigate *CONCORDE* from Newport. She brought three letters from General Rochambeau, and some American pilots from Newport. After reading the letters, de Grasse postponed the sailing of the merchant convoy to Europe and started planning to take his fleet to North America. Based on Gen. Rochambeau's recommendation, DeGrasse chose the Chesapeake as his destination---the critical decision that would bring the war's culmination to Virginia.

* * * * *

About the same time, at Barbados, British West Indies, Admiral George Rodney wrote Admiral Graves at New York, "...as the enemy has a fleet of 28 sail-of-the-line at Martinique, part of which is reported destined for North America, I am sending the *SWALLOW* to inform you that I shall keep a sharp lookout on their motions. If I send a squadron to North America, I shall order it to make landfall at the Capes of Virginia, then proceed to the Capes of Delaware, and from there to Sandy Hook, unless intelligence from you should require it to act otherwise.

Please order your Cruisers at the Chesapeake to look for it. I am informed the enemy squadron will sail in a short time: you may depend on the squadron in America being reinforced, should the enemy send their forces your way...." Because of the vagaries of wind, weather, and shipping, this communication did not arrive in New York until August 20th.

* * * * *

The disagreement between Clinton and Cornwallis over how to run the war heated up a little more on July 8th, when Clinton wrote from New York, "..I could not conceive you would require over 4000 troops in a station where Gen. Arnold told me 2000 would be ample. ...being strongly impressed with the necessity of our having a naval station for large ships, and judging Yorktown important for securing one, I cannot but be concerned that Your Lordship should suddenly lose sight of it, cross James River, and retire your army to the sickly post of Portsmouth....because you are of opinion that it exceeded your power, consistent with my plans, to make a safe post at York. "

"*My plans*, my Lord, were to draw from Chesapeake, as well for the sake of their health, as for the defense of *this* important post, such troops as *Your Lordship* could spare from a respectable defensive post at York, or other station as was proper to cover line-of-battle ships. I think Lafayette will seize and fortify York the moment he hears you have crossed the James, although he may be as unable to defend it with 5000 troops as you judge yourself to be."

"I would be sorry to begin with a siege the operation I am determined to carry on in the Chesapeake as soon as the season will permit. ...With regard to Portsmouth...when I sent Gen. Leslie to the Chesapeake [in October 1780], I only wanted a station to cover our cruising frigates, etc. He chose Portsmouth and had, I doubt not, good reasons for so doing. ...it has always been my opinion that if a better post for covering line-of-battle ships could be found, it ought to have preference. I think if Old Point Comfort will secure Hampton Roads, that is the station we ought to choose...with a small post at Mill Point. "

"*As for quitting the Chesapeake entirely*, I cannot entertain a thought of such a measure, but, on the contrary, as soon as the season will permit, shall most probably send there all the troops which can possibly be spared from the different posts under my command....even though Your Lordship has quitted York and detached troops to me, you should have a sufficiency to reoccupy it or you can at least hold Old Point Comfort, if it is possible to do it without York."[18]

In addition to setting Cornwallis straight, Clinton was writing for Lord Germain's benefit as Germain had recently said he agreed with Cornwallis that the Chesapeake and Virginia were of primary importance.

* * * * *

In London, the Lords Commissioners of the Admiralty, on July 9th, dispatched an order to Adm. Graves, in New York, "...You shall proceed in the *LONDON* to Jamaica to reinforce His Majesty's squadron on that station. ...on arrival, put yourself under command of Vice Admiral Sir Peter Parker. In case Adm. Arbuthnot has left and you are in command of the North Atlantic Squadron, you will turn it over to Rear Admiral Digby on his arrival."[9]

With this order, Graves was effectively relieved of command of the North Atlantic Squadron---almost sixty days before his fateful battle off the Virginia Capes, Sept. 5th. But, with communication by "swift sailing ship", he did not receive it, nor did Adm. Digby arrive New York, until after the battle.

In the West Indies, on the same day, Admiral Rodney messaged Adm. Samuel Hood, second in command, "...I have received intelligence that a considerable squadron of the enemy's line-of-battle ships is intended to reenforce the French squadron in America; and, it being absolutely necessary that a squadron of His Majesty's ships should reenforce his squadron in North America, You are directed to proceed immediately, with the ships *ALFRED, ALCIDE, INVINCIBLE, BARFLUER, MONARCH, PRINCE WILLIAM, RESOLUTION,* and *ST. MONICA* to the roads of St. Johns, Antigua where you will make every effort to compleat them with masts, cordage, and sails for a foreign voyage."[10]

* * * * *

On July 10th Rochambeau finally advised Washington he had written DeGrasse that, in view of prevailing winds, it would be the best plan to go to the Chesapeake, "...in which he could do great work on the naval forces found there, the prevailing wind then bringing him on to New York.". He also pleaded with DeGrasse to bring soldiers and money.[11]

* * * * *

In Suffolk, Va., on the same day, Earl Cornwallis sent a message to Gen. Leslie, in Portsmouth, " I do not want any more provisions landed until I arrive at Portsmouth.". He also called for troops to be sent him in boats, if they could be manned without calling on the ships scheduled for sea, if not, they were to march. ...the Regiment of Prince Hereditaire was to send 60 of the marchers to the Great Bridge; a detachment of the 80th was ordered to Kemp's Landing, while the 17th was to take post at Portsmouth. He ended with, "...the news from Great Britain gives me a great pleasure."[1] [this refers to the letter from Lord Germain saying he was doing the right thing.]

From New York, on the 11th, Gen. Clinton wrote Cornwallis, "...I have conferred with Admiral Graves: ...we are both of opinion it is absolutely necessary we should hold a station in Chesapeake Bay for ships-of-the-line as well as frigates. The Admiral thinks that if the enemy holds Old Point Comfort, Elizabeth River would no longer be of use to us . We therefore judge Hampton Roads to be the fittest station for all ships. ...it is moreover, my opinion that possession of Yorktown, even though we did not possess Gloucester, might give security to any works we might have at Old Point, which I understand secures Hampton Roads. ...Please lose no time in examining Old Point and fortify it , obtaining such troops as you think necessary for that purpose and garrisoning it afterwards."[2]

Clinton continues that if he thinks it necessary to keep all 7,000 men, he could: this should indicate the importance he gave to a naval station in the Chesapeake. ..he saw no necessity for holding Portsmouth. Cornwallis did not receive that letter until July 21st.

On the 13th, Gen. Leslie informed Cornwallis the embarkation from Portsmouth was in a great state of forwardness...with horse transports for 300 horses and 2800 men. He asked if the guns and mortars should be loaded, or remain at Portsmouth. Leslie followed up on the 14th with word that the transports were loaded and falling down river in order to get under way on the 15th. ...they were short shipping for one regiment.

In New York, on the 15th, Clinton, showing his growing irritation, fired off another letter to Cornwallis in answer to Cornwallis's letter of the 8th. He had hoped Cornwallis would wait on the Peninsula side for a letter from him, as they both seemed to agree on the propriety of taking a healthy station in the neck between York and James River, in order to cover a proper harbor for line-of-battle ships. "...As you point out the question of a defensive post in Virginia, which cannot have much influence on the war in Carolina, and only gives some acres of unhealthy swamp, I must beg leave again to repeat that it never was my intention to continue a post on Elizabeth any longer than necessary, until the commencement of solid operations in the Chesapeake...and, that all General Officers who have commanded in Chesapeake Bay have had my consent to change that station for one more healthy, if they judged it proper to do so."

"I will add, it always has been, is, and ever will be, my firm opinion, that it is of the utmost consequence to His Majesty's affairs on this continent, that we take possession of the Chesapeake, and that we do not afterwards relinquish it. ...with respect to the unhealthiness of Portsmouth, my letters to Gen. Phillips state, 'God forbid, I should wish to bury the elite of my army in Nansemond and Princess Anne', that should satisfy you that we are both of the same opinion."[18]

* * * * *

At Cape Francois, Hispaniola [Cape Haitian, Haiti], Admiral DeGrasse was joined by Chevalier Monteil's squadron on July 15th. On the way to the Bahamas Channel, DeGrasse lost two ships to odd accidents: L'Aine, cook on *AUGUSTE* described one,"...while storekeepers onboard *INTREPIDE* were transferring liquor, one dropped a candle. Fire broke out immediately and caught the whole ship. All they did was useless, and they hastened to beach the ship. They threw most of the powder into the sea and wetted the remainder, but the heat evaporated the humidity;---the ship blew up at 11 o'clock. The commotion was terrible; all the houses in town were shaken. One cannot describe the fright!"[19] This occurred at Cape Island, St. Domingo.

Loading artillery on AUGUSTE
at Cap Francois, Haiti
Courtesy La Neptune, Paris

Explosion onboard French ship INTREPIDE,
at Cape Island, St. Domingo, caused by
a fire resulting from spilled cognac.

Courtesy La Neptune, Paris

* * * * *

Back in Portsmouth, on the 17th, Gen Leslie sent a boat to Capt. Hudson, anchored off Old Point, advising him not to take his ships to sea until further word came from Lord Cornwallis. The same day, he wrote Gen. Clinton that the embarkation would be completed that afternoon. "...the delay was caused by having to fit out three supply ships as transports. ...nothing has been wanting on my part to expedite this business."[11] He also sent a rider off to Cornwallis with a just arrived letter from Gen. Clinton, Leslie added one of his own which said everything was being held up until he heard back from him after Cornwallis had an opportunity to read Clinton's latest.

On the 20th, Cornwallis answered Leslie's message of the 19th; "...by a letter I received from the Commander-in-Chief, it is necessary to stop the sailing of the expedition, which you will please do, and remain with the transports in Hampton Roads until you hear further from me. Please communicate this to the Commodore."[11] Cornwallis arrived in Portsmouth on July 25th and was greeted with a cannonade salute.

* * * * *

At Newport, R.I., July 20th; Gen. Rochambeau asked Washington for a campaign plan that could be sent to Adm. deGrasse. Because of uncertainties with enlistments and drafts from the states, Washington was reluctant to give a detailed plan. He said he would prepare for the primary objective of a movement against New York, as agreed at Weathersfield; secondly, for some action in the South, if, after de Grasse's arrival, he found he did not have sufficient men and equipent for a New York venture.

On the 21st, Washington wrote de Grasse advising him of the New York situation. This letter was given to Gen. David Foreman who was sent to Sandy Hook on the New Jersey coast to await the arrival of the French fleet and deliver it to Adm. de Grasse. Although advised by Rochambeau that de Grasse would probably head for the Chesapeake, Washington still hoped to focus the campaign on New York.

Adms. Rodney and Hood conferring onboard
H.M.S. Gibraltar in the Leeward Islands
just before Rodney turns over command and
sails for England.

Courtesy La Neptune, Paris

* * * * *

In the West Indies, on the 24th, Sir George Rodney directed Admiral Hood to take the convoy to St. Eustatius and St. Kitts, then head for Cape Tiberon, Jamaica, then proceed with the remainder of the line to the coast of North America, where he should employ them in protecting the friends of His Majesty and harassing his enemies. As he had previously advised the Commanding Officer at New York, by the *SWALLOW*, that the West Indies ships would make the Capes of Virginia first, then the Capes of Delaware, then Sandy Hook, Hood's course should conform.

Unfortunately, for the British, Adm. Graves was at sea when the *SWALLOW* arrived in New York. Gen. Clinton sent another ship northward to look for Graves, but, they never met; consequently, Graves did not learn of Rodney's plans until August 20th. Rodney had enclosed intelligence that a French frigate had arrived at Cap Francois on July 10th with 30 ship's pilots from the Chesapeake, which indicated the French fleet was eagerly awaited in North America. Actually, Rodney's intelligence was wrong---the pilots were not from the Chesapeake, but from Newport. The ship, *CONCORDE*, was carrying letters from Gen. Rochambeau.

* * * * *

The disagreement between Cornwallis and Clinton becomes more open on July 23rd when Lord Cornwallis wrote Lord Rawdon, in Charleston, "...I have not time to explain my situation; suffice it to say that the Commander-in-Chief is determined to throw all blame on me, and to disapprove of all I have done. ...nothing but conscience can induce me to remain. I offered to return to Carolina; but, it was not approved." [18]

On the 24th, it escalates again when Cornwallis wrote his Commander-in-Chief, "by yours of May 29th, I find that my march to Wilmington, nor to Petersburg, met with your approval. In neither of those, did I risk my Corps or that of General Phillips, as I would have returned to Wilmington had I not heard from Phillips that I could join him in safety. With the warmest zeal for King and Country, I am aware my judgement is liable to error. Perhaps my measures were not the best; but, at least, I have the satisfaction to find, by captured letters from Gen. Greene to Gen. Steuben, that Greene did not want me in Virginia."[1]

Aboard *H.M.S. RICHMOND,* in Hampton Roads, July 25th; Captains Hudson, Symonds, and Everett advised Gen. Cornwallis, "...in response to the request from the Commander-in-Chief relative to a post at Old Point Comfort to protect the King's ships, ...we have examined that place as close as possible and are unanimously of opinion that, from the width of the channel and depth of water close to it, any superior enemy force coming in, could pass any work established there, with little damage, or destroy it and any ships anchored there under its protection."[1]

Lt. Sutherland, an engineering officer in Cornwallis's command, had accompanied the Captains and concurred, adding, "...the ground is not two feet above mean high water which means, with the short distance to deep water, destruction by naval attack. Passing ships have no reason to come within range of arms. The time and expense needed to build a fort would be considerable because earth for ramparts and parapets, and all other material, must be carried in as there are none there." [About 100 years prior to this, July 1666, Thomas Ludwell, of Virginia, advised the Earl of Clarendon, of the King's Council, of the same problems with fortifying Old Point Comfort. JHR]

On the 27th, Capt. Hudson wrote Admiral Graves, "...Earl Cornwallis and I, and others, are of opinion Old Point Comfort is not a place to erect a Post, at or near, for the protection of the King's ships. We have come to a resolution to remove the troops now at Portsmouth and vicinity to York and Gloucester where we believe a better Post can be established for protection of the King's troops. This prevents Lord Cornwallis from sending any troops to New York immediately, as all ships will be used in the transfer"[1]

The same day, Cornwallis sent off a lengthy letter to Gen. Clinton, trying to straighten out the misunderstanding of Clinton's orders and Cornwallis's intentions. "...I shall, in obedience to the spirit of Your Excellency's orders, take measures , as quickly as possible, to seize and fortify York and Gloucester, being the only harbor in which we can hope to be able to give effective protection to line-of-battle ships. I shall also evacuate Portsmouth and the posts belonging to it. *...until that is accomplished,* it will be impossible for me to spare troops, as York and Gloucester command no countryside and a superiority in the field will be necessary to enable us to draw forage and other supplies from the countryside, and to carry on our works without interruption. ..."[1]

* * * * *

From the Caribbean, on the 28th, Admiral DeGrasse wrote Gen. Rochambeau, "...I bring with me in all 3000 men, 100 artillarists, 100 dragoons, 10 campaign cannons, and siege guns; they will be embarked on 25 or 26 men-of-war which will set out on August 3rd to make the Chesapeake as soon as possible---which seems to me the place indicated by Rochambeau, Washington, Luzerne and Barras as the most desirable. I will be obliged to you for employing me promptly and effectively in order that the time be sufficiently well employed. ...I cannot leave you the troops ...as they are under orders of the Spanish General who is preparing for a winter campaign in Florida. ...this entire expedition has been arranged following your orders, and as it was impossible to communicate with either the French or Spanish Ministers, I believe myself authorized to take over responsibilities in view of the common good; but, I dare not entirely change the plan of their project by transplanting such a considerable corps of men."

"I read with sadness of the distress in which the Americans find themselves and the need of prompt aid....I conferred with M. de Lilliancourt who has taken command of the government and have induced him to give me, from the garrison at Saint Domingue, the regiments of Gatinais, Agenois, and Tourtaine. ...." [1]

In a <u>copy</u> sent to DeBarras, DeGrasse added, "...I leave you free to decide whether you should come to join me or operate on your coast for the common good. Keep me informed." DeGrasse had difficulty raising the money asked for by Rochambeau and Washington. In spite of offering to pledge his personal real estate in Saint Domingue and France, the merchants and bankers would not advance the money. Finally, DeGrasse approached the Spanish Minister at Cap Francois, Senor de Salvedra, and succeeded in convincing him to raise the 1,200,000 livres in Havana.

* * * * *

At Malvern Hill, Virginia, on July 28th, Gen. Lafayette wrote Col. Parker, at Smithfield, "...there is something puzzling in the delay of the enemy fleet in Hampton Roads. ...is it possible for you to find out what detains them? ...will it not be safe to move nearer to the enemy lines to ascertain their intentions, and improve the opportunity of injuring them, should a general embarkation take place?" [54]

Lafayette also wrote Gen. Washington, "...for sometime, we have been reporting that the embarkation from Portsmouth was designed to go up the Bay: ...Baltimore being particularly mentioned. Commodore Barron, who is watching their motions, writes that on the 30th, 40 sail weighed from Hampton Roads, with 12 barges full of men, and stood towards the Capes; but, having gained the proper channel, tried to stand up the Bay. The wind not being favorable, they anchored. ...it is reported that troops of Earl Cornwallis's army, under Gen. O'Hara, landed in Gloucester Co., near the mouth of the York, and are erecting fortifications." [1]

In Newport, on the 30th, Washington received a letter from Adm. de Barras: he was reluctant to leave Newport until Adm. de Grasse arrived. Washington again realized that his French allies were not enthusiastic for an attack on New York. He started considering an action in the south. Gen. Knox was asked to make plans for a move. Mr. Morris, in Philadelphia, was asked to look into the availability of shipping from Head of Elk river, Md. to the lower Chesapeake Bay. [1]

* * * * *

At St. Eustatius, Dutch West Indies, Adm. George Rodney turned over command of the West Indies fleet to Adm. Samuel Hood, and sailed for England with his convoy of merchant ships and prizes taken at that island. Before sailing he suggested that Hood recall Adm. Drake and his squadron from St. Lucia and take them with him to North America. Hood sailed for St. Johns, Antiqua after sending a message to Drake to join him there. After waiting a week for Drake, Hood sailed from St. Johns on August 10th: Drake's squadron met Hood's just off the island.

In Yorktown, Virginia, August 2, 1781; Lt. Gen. Earl Cornwallis wrote Brig Gen. O'Hara, in Portsmouth; "...after a passage of four days, we landed here and at Gloucester. The position is bad and we need more troops. ...As you know, every senior officer takes, without remorse, from a junior, and tells him he has nothing to fear...send me more troops."[1]

That same day, in New York, Gen. Clinton sent off another letter to his Second in Command, Gen. Cornwallis; "...as it was not my intention to give offense, and it is extremely my wish to be clearly understood by Your Lordship....from the moment you took charge of a separate command, I left you at full liberty to act in it as you judged best for the King's service. I have constantly pursued this line of conduct...having no other objective than diligently listening to your wants and supplying them. ...I was content to remain here upon the very confined defensive to which I was reduced by the large detachments I sent southward in support of your progress: I left with you in Charleston in 1780, 6400 troops, sent under Leslie-2800, sent with Arnold-2200, sent with Phillips-2700, reenforced-900, total 14,900."
"I fear the advantages resulting from your junction with the Chesapeake Army will not compensate for the losses which immediately followed your quitting Carolina. ...I spared no pains to explain my desires to Your Lordship, though I have, perhaps, unhappily failed in making them understood. ...Based on your letter of May 26th, in which you said you had re-

viewed the papers of Gen. Phillips, had the same objections to Portsmouth, and thought well of York as a proper harbor and place of arms, I concluded Your Lordship entirely concurred with me...and I supposed Your Lordship would set about establishing yourself there immediately on your return from Richmond. ...therefore, imagining Your Lordship well advanced in your works (as I had no further communication until June 30th), I solicited you for a part of your force to assist me in the operation planned for this quarter.."

"In my letter of June 19th, I said, 'I cannot but wish...that you send me, as soon as possible, what you can spare from a respectable defensive, it is necessary to inform you, that other intelligence, than M. de Barras letter, makes it highly probable that M. De Grasse will visit this coast in the hurricane season, and bring with him troops as well as ships.' After this very candid and ample explanation, My Lord, I have only to assure you it was not my intention to pass the slightest censure on Your Lordship's conduct, much less an unmerited or severe one. ...perhaps my language was more positive than I had been accustomed to use to Your Lordship; but, I had no objective in view than to make myself clearly understood."[11]

Such a lengthy apology from a Commanding Officer to a Subordinate clearly indicates the problems Clinton faced in prosecuting his strategy for winning the war. In England, the Nobility controlled the Government—and the armed forces. Being one of them, Cornwallis went around Clinton to Clinton's superiors with impunity. After receiving several missives from Lord George Germain, in which he sided with Earl Cornwallis, Clinton, obviously, became more concerned with being misunderstood, or in offending, than in having his directives carried out. By his actions, Cornwallis greatly affected the conduct of the war. [This controversy continued for years after the war.]

* * * * *

That same day, Aug. 2nd, Gen. Washington wrote in his diary that after reviewing the situation of getting new levies for his forces, and the probable arrival of reinforcement for the British in New York, he had decided to forego an attack on New York and turn his view southward. This decision was no doubt affected by what Gen. Rochambeau had told him about his letters to Adm. De Grasse. He wrote Robert Morris, in Philadelphia, asking what shipping could be collected there and at Baltimore, by August 20th, for transporting troops and supplies down the Bay.[1]

According to a French Journal, at 3 A.M. on August 5th, Admiral De Grasse signalled his fleet to raise kedge anchors and heave short on the large anchors: at 5 A.M., he signalled to begin rigging, and shortly afterwards the fleet got under way. De Grasse plotted a course through the Bermuda channel for two reasons: first, to rendezvous with the *AIGRETTE* which had gone to Havana to pick up the 1,200,000 livres raised by the Spanish, for the Americans; also, to mislead and stay clear of any British ships. He took on Spanish pilots to get him through the channel. On the 7th, De Grasse was joined by *CITOYEN, HERCULE, EXPERIMENT,* and a frigate. De Grasse's fleet now numbered 28. On the 8th, *GLORIEUX* and *SOUVERAIN* joined up. Shortly afterward, they sighted Cuba.[1b]

CHAPTER SEVEN

Head for the Chesapeake and Virginia:

From Pamunky River, Lafayette wrote Washington on August 6th, "...instead of continuing his voyage up the Bay, my Lord entered York River, landing at York and Gloucester. His Lordship maneuvers so well no blunder can be hoped for, to recover a bad step by us. ...York is surrounded by the river and a morass. The entrance is narrow. There is a commanding hill which, if the enemy occupies it, would much extend their works. ...their vessels, the biggest a forty-four, are between the two towns. Should a French fleet come at this time, our affairs would take a happy turn. "[1]

* * * * *

H.M.S. RICHMOND, York River, August 12th, Capt. Hudson to Admiral Graves, New York: "...arrived here with *CHARON, GUADALOUPE, BONETTA, SWIFT, LOYAL-IST*, and all transports, with 4500 men. Left *FOWEY and VULCAN* at Portsmouth. The Earl asked if I would order the guns from the ships to be placed at Gloucester, which I did. Gloucester is now pretty heavily fortified. Capt. Robinson says it will take 10 days to destroy the works and evacuate Portsmouth. I have stationed *BONETTA* at Lynnhaven to inform any friends who may come in, of the situation."[1]

* * * * *

Newport Harbor, August 12th: the French frigate *CONCORDE* arrives from the West Indies with dispatches for Rochambeau and de Barras. Barras tells Rochambeau that De Grasse did not call for him to come to the Chesapeake, so he thought he would sail for Halifax, Nova Scotia. Washington and Rochambeau were taken by surprise with this, but, after much persuasion, finally got Barras to wait, then agree to take the siege cannon to the Chesapeake.

* * * * *

H.M.S. GIBRALTAR, at sea, August 13th; Admiral Rodney to Admiral in Command, New York: "...when I left St. Eustasia, Admiral Hood was preparing to sail with 12 ship-of-the-line, 4 frigates, and one fire ship, for the Capes of Virginia where, I am persuaded, the French intend making a grand effort. I recommend you collect all your forces and join Hood there. I hope you will have heard of Hood's coming prior to this, via his frigate. ...When de Grasse left Grenada he had 26 sail-of-the-line and two ships armed "en flute". ...Hood is to return immediately after the full moon of October."[1]

There is no apparent explanation why Rodney waited so long to forward the intelligence on deGrasse ---he received it on July 31st. Hood's frigate did not arrive New York until August 20th: Rodney's courier, later, Sept. 8th---after the Battle Off the Capes.

* * * * *

In his diary for August 14th, General Washington wrote, "...matters having come to a crisis, and a decisive plan needed, I was obliged, from the short-ness of Count de Grasse's stay on this coast, ...and the inability to get drafts from the states, to give up all idea of attacking New York, and, instead, to remove the French troops and a detachment of the American Army to the Head of the Elk River, to be transported to Virginia, in order to cooperate with the forces from the West Indies against the British troops there. ..."[1]

For the second time, Washington acknowledges that, although he preferred New York as the main theater of the war, circumstances, actually Rochambeau's suggestions to DeGrasse, are making it necessary to shift his attention and operations to Virginia.

The same day, Washington wrote Lafayette, in Virginia, telling him to seek means to open communica-tion with de Grasse, on his arrival, and to combine efforts with him for the use of joint forces, until he received additional support from the Northward.

* * * * *

From Yorktown, Cornwallis wrote Clinton on the 16th; "...the evacuation of Portsmouth has employed an engineer and a number of laborers and artificers; with every effort by land and water, I do not expect the work to be completed before the 21st... . After our experience with the labor and difficulty of constructing works at this season, and the plan for fortifying this side not entirely settled, I cannot, at present, tell you whether I can spare any troops, or if any, how soon..."[1] At this time, the Troops in Virginia under command of Lt. Gen. Earl Cornwallis, numbered as follows, 5177 British, 2112 German, and 839 American Provincials: 8128 were enlisted, 259 officers, with staff, chaplains, surgeons and mates, total over 8500.

* * * * *

On August 17th, Washington wrote de Grasse suggesting alternatives for the cooperation between their forces, depending on what the British did; ...if they left their forces at York, York should be attacked. If they split their forces, sending some to Charleston, Charleston should be attacked. If some were sent to New York, they would have to decide what to do when they met. He asked de Grasse to send as many ships as possible up the Bay to the Head of the Elk River and Baltimore in order that the Americans and French could be brought down.[1]

In the Caribbean, on the same day, the French sighted land at Matanzas, Cuba: the *HECTOR* joined up, bringing the total fleet to 28 ship-of-the-line, 3 frigates, and 3 cutters. At daybreak on the 18th, the *AIGRETTE* joined, bringing the 1,200,000 livres borrowed from the people of Havana. De Grass signalled for all Spanish pilots to be brought to the *VILLE DE PARIS*, from which, they were returned to Havana. At 4 PM the fleet set sail for the Bahamas Channel.[11]

The combined forces of Washington and Rochambeau crossed the Hudson River on August 18th---supposedly to position for an attack on New York; actually, it was the start of the march to Virginia.

From the Forks of the York River, on August 21, Gen. Lafayette wrote to Gen. Washington; "...from the enemy's preparations , I should infer they are working for the protection of their fleet, and for defense against another....from their cautious and partial moves, I should conclude their intelligence is not too good. ...I hope you will come yourself to Virginia, and that, if the French army moves this way, I shall have the satisfaction of beholding you at the head of the combined armies. Lord Cornwallis must be attacked with a pretty great apparatus; but, when a French fleet takes possession of the Bay and rivers, and our land force is superior to his, his army must, sooner or later, be forced to surrender, as we may get what reinforcements we may need. ...I heartily thank you for having ordered me to remain in Virginia. "[*]

* * * * *

In Yorktown, on the 22nd, Cornwallis messaged Gen. Clinton; "...Portsmouth is evacuated. Gen. O'Hara arrived here today with the stores and troops. ...a great number of refugees from Norfolk and Princess Anne Counties, and Suffolk accompanied him. ...the engineer has completed his plan for the defense of this place and I have ordered it executed. ...I will not take any step that will retard the establishing of this post; but, I request you decide whether it is more important that a detachment of 1000 or 1200 men be sent to you or kept here with the rest of the troops to expedite the completion of the works."

"Lafayette is at Fork of the York with his Continentals plus a large body of 18 months state troops [short-term draftees], and two brigades of militia under Stevens and Lawson. He has armed 400 of the Virginia prisoners lately arrived from Charleston, and expects to be joined soon by Gen. Smallwood, with 700 18 months men from Maryland: Wayne and Morgan, now on this side of the James, march to join him."[**]

* * * * *

According to Tornquist, a Dane fighting with the French fleet, on the 23rd, they were abeam of Charleston; Weather was squally with thunderstorms. They captured two British vessels; CORMORANT--24 guns, and QUEEN CHARLOTTE--18. On board the last, was Lord Rawdon and a number of loyalists.[13]

*****

On August 24th, General Henry Knox advised
Gen. Washington of the ordnance which would go south
with the American army; siege guns, 3-24s, 20-18s,
2-8" mortars, 3-8" howitzers, 10-10" mortars, 2-12"
howitzers, 6-6s, 3-5s, all brass.

That same day, Adm. de Barras's squadron left
Newport Harbor for the Chesapeake, carrying the siege
guns---he went so far out to sea, to avoid any British
patrols, he did not arrive at the Chesapeake until
Sept. 10th, five days after the battle off the Capes.

*****

Admiral Hood's fleet made a landfall just south
of Cape Henry, Virginia on August 25th; he dispatched
a "fast sailing ship" to New York to advise Admiral
Graves of his coming, and also sent a frigate into the
Chesapeake to look for the French. On being signaled,
'no french ships sighted', Hood ordered, "continue on
course for New York", as instructed by Adm. Rodney.

*****

At Sandy Hook,[N.J.] Gen. David Forman, who was
keeping a coastal watch for British warships, sent a
messenger off to Generals Washington and Rochambeau
that a British fleet of 13 ships had gone inside the
bar on the 27th of August. This was Adm. Hood's. Hood
went ashore to meet with Gen. Clinton and Adm. Graves
who were discussing an attack on the French fleet of
Adm. de Barras, at Newport. Hood urged Graves to
combine forces and go after the French to the south-
ward---Graves agreed. They were Talking of seeking
and attacking De Grasse's fleet, only,---at this time,
they did not know of Washington and Rochambeau's
plan to march to Virginia for an attack on Cornwallis.

*****

The fleet of Adm. De Grasse arrived off the
mouth of the Chesapeake on August 28th and anchored
about three leagues from Cape Henry. On the 29th,
they entered the Bay and anchored in Lynnhaven
Roads. Shortly afterward, a local vessel, with tories

onboard, approached, hailed, and asked for Admiral Hood. An english speaking French sailor talked them into coming aboard where they were taken prisoners. The fruit and fresh vegetables brought as a gift for Hood were eaten by De Grasse and his staff.

The weather in Chesapeake Bay was good on the 30th. De Grasse signalled for the debarkation of the troops of Saint-Simon, a good part of whom, were loaded into ship's boats and carried up the James to the Chickahominey River. French frigates were busy capturing English ships in the Bay. At the anchorage, Gen. Duportail, French engineer on Washington's staff, presented dispatches to Adm. De Grasse; in one, Washington asked that all the frigates and transports that could be spared be sent up the Bay to Head of the Elk River and Baltimore to pick up his troops.[11]

On the same day, Washington, Rochambeau, and Knox rode into Philadelphia, ahead of the army. They were greeted with cheers and wined and dined. General Henry Knox told the Board of War that Washington had directed him to collect all the arms and accouterments available, to be carried southward.

* * * * *

On the 31st,, at Yorktown, Cornwallis wrote his Commander-in-Chief, "..a Lieutenant of the *CHARON* went with an escort of Dragoons to Old Point Comfort. ...he reports there were between thirty and forty sail within the Capes, mostly ships of war...some large."[10]

The same day, at New York, Admiral Graves wrote Phillip Stephens, in London, that his squadron finally got over the bar at Sandy Hook and was proceeding southward with that of Adm. Hood. The *PRINCESSA* logged "...under-way at 5 PM." Included in Graves squadron were the ships-of-the-line, *LONDON, BEDFORD, ROYAL OAK, EUROPE, AMERICA, ADAMANT,* and *frigates, NYMPHE, SOLEBAY, AND RICHMOND.*[1]

* * * * *

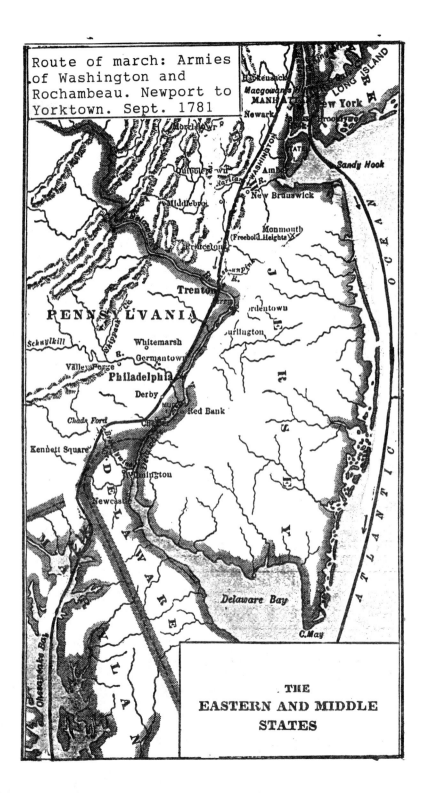

Route of march: Armies of Washington and Rochambeau. Newport to Yorktown. Sept. 1781

THE
EASTERN AND MIDDLE
STATES

Dawn of Sept 2nd found the French ships in Lynnhaven Bay continuing the debarkation of Saint-Simons troops and carrying them up James River where they went ashore near Jamestown to join Lafayette's Corps. On the Bay, *GLORIEUX* patrolled the mouth of the York River. *AIGRETTE* rejoined the fleet, bringing two British ships she had captured. Aboard *VILLE DE PARIS* Admiral De Grasse and Gen. Duportail were planning strategy for a combined operation against Cornwallis at York. De Grasse sent a ship up the Bay with messages for Washington and Rochambeau telling of his arrival. The ship went to Baltimore where Gen. Gist, of the Maryland Milita, dispatched a rider to the Head of the Elk with the news.

On the same day, a North Carolina Militia Colonel, John Wells, notified General Jones of the arrival of the French Fleet at Cape Henry and a rumor that Cornwallis was planning to cross James River and fight his way into North Carolina and back to Wilmington.[11]

In Lynnhaven Bay, A french Officer, deGoussencourt, almost drowned when his ship's boat capsized while going ashore; fortunately it had struck a sand-bar, so they were able to stand and walk ashore. He noted in his diary that the countryside was beautiful , with fine woods, large houses, pastures covered with cattle, and creeks jumping with fish. L'Aine, the French cook, wrote that parties going ashore for fresh water dug a hole in the sand and sunk a barrel; soon water filled the barrel and they drank. About five miles inland, a market had been set up to service the fleet: prices were reasonable and fish, fresh meat, poultry, and vegetables abounded.[11]

* * * * *

Off the Jersey shore, 70 miles from Sandy Hook, the British *PRINCESSA* logged, "...weather good with almost 'following winds'. Orders to exercise the great guns and small arms." By noon of the 2nd. she had logged, "...120 miles from Sandy Hook; weather was fair, winds light, and still following."[11]

At New York, Sir Henry Clinton wrote Gen. Cornwallis; "...from intelligence I have received, it seems Washington is moving his Army to the southward, in haste, and says he expects the cooperation of a considerable French armament. Your Lordship may be assured that I shall endeavor to reinforce the army under your command by all means possible---or make every possible move in your favor. ...Capt. Stanhope, of the *PEGASUS*, just arrived from the West Indies, says that on last Friday, about sixty leagues off the coast, he was chased by eight ships-of-the-line, which he took to be French: they counted forty sail in all. HOWEVER,as Admiral Graves, joined by Sir Samuel Hood with 14 copper bottomed ships, sailed from here on the 31st, with 19 ship-of-the-line, plus some 50s. I flatter myself you will have little to fear from that of the French (19 against 28). Washington is reported to be marching to Head of the Elk where they will take boats to the Bay. If navigation is interrupted, he will go by land from Baltimore. Your Excellency can best judge the time required---I should suppose about three weeks from Trenton. He has about 4000 French troops and about 2000 Rebels with him."[18]

On the 2nd, at Yorktown, Cornwallis messaged Clinton: "...Comte de Grasse's fleet is within the Capes of the Chesapeake. Forty boats with troops went up the James River yesterday, and four ships lie at the entrance of this river." In a later message he noted, "..the French fleet consists of 17 sail-of-the-line."[18]

* * * * *

In Philadelphia, while marching through town, the American troops found that some would have to continue their march to Annapolis and Baltimore, rather than Head of the Elk. Robert Morris, Secretary of the Treasury, had been able to borrow 30,000 "hard dollars" from General Rochambeau, so the Americans got an unexpected payday---in cold cash!

While in Philadelphia, Washington wrote Lafayette, "...the present time is as interesting and anxious a moment as I have ever experienced. We will hope, however, for the most propitious issue of our united exertions. ...the whole French Army and the American Corps is now marching with Major General Benjamin Lincoln. [former commander of American forces at Charleston, S.C., who had to surrender his force in May 1780. He was freed in a prisoner exchange.] With the addition of the land forces expected on the fleet, I hope we shall not experience any considerable difficulty from the want of men to carry out our most favorable project. ...General Knox is making every exertion to have an adequate supply of heavy cannon, ordnance stores and ammunition... ."[8]

As the French troops marched through town in their colorful uniforms, they were greeted with cheers.

* * * * *

In Hampton Roads, Admiral de Grasse wrote Washington, "...I am poorly equipped with ships to be used as transports to help you in transporting your troops down the Bay. ...I fear that the time at my disposal will not permit me to give all the aid to the United States which I should wish. I had resolved to attack York with the Marquis's troops and those which I brought in my ships; but because of the letter which I received from Your Excellency, and on the advise of Duportail, I have suspended my plans until the arrival of the Generals whose experience in the profession of arms, knowledge of the country, and insight will greatly augment our resources. ...I could give, in case of need, 1800 men of good troops, from the garrison of the fleet, and I can furnish land and siege cannons. These can only be fired from gun rests, but their balls create quite as much disturbance."[11]

* * * * *

At Chester Pennsylvannia, on September 4th, General George Washington and his staff got news of the arrival of Admiral DeGrasse's fleet in the Chesapeake and that seige guns were being unloaded and sent to Lafayette at Williamsburg: one report said that Washington was so excited," he almost danced a jig." On arrival at the Head of Elk River, they found a shortage of shipping. After a conference, Washington and Rochambeau agreed to embark part of the troops there and take the balance on to Baltimore.

On the Chesapeake the weather was fine, wind fresh, sea calm. Adm. de Grasse ordered *AIGRETTE* and *SOUVRAIN* to cruise outside the Capes. Feeling the urgency of the situation, de Grasse sent a courier to Washington, "...I regard your arrival of such importance that I am doing the impossible to hasten that of your troops...by sending six or seven men-of-war from the fleet, which draw the least water, they will be followed by frigates and any other ships fit to mount the river. ...I am leaving on them only those sailors necessary to handle them. In that way they can carry more of your troops. ...I urge you to allow on board only those effects which are absolutely necessary."[1]

* * * * *

At sea, *HMS SHREWSBURY* logged, "...noon, wind SW, course S 80 W,weather fresh breezes and cloudy, Cape Charles S 28 W 66 miles, at 7 PM weather turned squally with lightening and rain."[2]

* * * * *

With the two fleets only 66 miles apart, lookout ships patrolling, and crews anticipating action, the stage was now set for the Battle Off The Capes of Virginia:

CHAPTER EIGHT

BEAR DOWN AND ENGAGE:

Dawn, September 5th, found the British frigate *SOLEBAY* on lookout in the southwest. The French frigate *AIGRETTE* patrolled just outside the Capes.

PRINCESSA logged, "...hoisted top gallant sails, let out second reefs in top sails. 29 sail of our fleet in sight. Cape Charles West by North-8 leagues (24 miles)".[11]

At 9AM:

LONDON, Adm. Graves flagship, logged; "...water depth 16 fathoms. Cape Henry West 6 leagues (18 mi.). *SOLEBAY* signaled a fleet in the southwest. Admiral signaled, prepare for action, called in all cruisers."[1]

ALCIDE, "...hoisted mizzen top gallant sails, 'clewed up' [rolled up] mainsail."[14]

Outside Cape Henry, *AIGRETTE sighted* a number of ships bearing down to the Capes. Recognizing that the fleet was too large to be de Barras's, she hoisted her signal flags and fired a gun. [16]

Aboard French *AUGUSTE,* Adm. Bouganville, hearing the signal gun, ordered his lookouts aloft.

Aboard *VILLE DE PARIS,* Adm. de Grasse ordered his flags to half-mast and fired a signal cannon to recall all ships boats. Gave signal to ready for combat and prepare to get underway.[11]

9:15 A.M.

AIGRETTE signalled, "27 sail bearing down form north-east."[16]

10 A.M:

LONDON, course SWbyW, discovered fleet of large ships at anchor near Cape Henry. made signal for line of battle ahead at 2 cable lengths [about 1200 ft].[1]

BARFLUER, Adm. Samuel Hood's flagship, "...*BED-FORD* made signal for 16 sail in SW quarter. Adm. made signal to prepare for action, we repeated...and cleared ship for action." At this time, *BARFLUER* was one of the Van, or lead, ships in the British fleet.[9]

ALCIDE, saw land bearing NW 7 or 8 leagues [22 miles], Cape Charles WNW 4-5 leagues. Adm. made signal to prepare for action.[14]

PRINCESSA, in the rear guard of the British, logged, "...26 sail of large ships at anchor in the southwest. repeated Admiral's signal for line of battle ahead at two cable lengths [1200 ft. apart] ..."[11]

French *MARSEILLAIS,* "6 sail in the east---then 25 sail. Adm. made signal to clear decks for action, and return all boats promptly."[11]

DeGoussencourt, onboard   , "..two frigates outside signalled sails in sight proved to be English, orders given to hoist sail."[11]

Tornquist, on *ZELE,* "...decided sails were enemy---all on starboard tack. We cleared for action."[11]

Aboard *LESCEPTRE,* Adm. Vauderuil noted, "...the British must have first thought we were the fleet of DeBarras, much smaller."[11]

10:30 A.M.

SHREWSBURY, "Admiral made signal to prepare for action and clear ship."[16]

BARFLUER, "Admiral made signal for *NYMPHE* to come to "hail". Repeated signal for line ahead at 2 cable lengths asunder."[9]

11 AM:

LONDON, "...forming line ahead and standing for Lynnhaven Bay. Clearing ship---preparing for action. Cape Henry west by south 3 leagues (9 mi.)" Weather moderate.[*LONDON* was at center of the British line.]"[9]

BARFLUER, "...set our studding sails."[9]

ALCIDE, ".signal for line ahead 2 cable lengths."[9]

11:30 AM:

SHREWSBURY,"..land WNW 4-5 leagues [12-15 miles]."[16]

Onboard French *AUGUSTE*, cook L'Aine, diaried, "...Adm. de Grasse signals ships that cannot raise anchors to run out their cables and buoy the lines. We cut one of ours."[18]

Frenchman deGoussencourt wrote,"...orders given to slip cables and leave buoys"[11].

French journalist, Jenout, noted, "...One frigate from enemy fired a cannon. *AIGRETTE* signals 23 ships. Adm. de Grasse is careful."[18]

12:00 NOON:

BARFLUER, "...all the fleet in company. Cape Henry west by south, two leagues [6 mi.]." After the battle, Adm. Hood wrote, "...French came out in line of battle---close hauled, but by no means regular or connected; affording us a glorious opportunity to make a close attack. But, it was not taken." [9]

SHREWSBURY, "Cape Charles NWbyW 4 leagues [12 miles]. French starting to come out of the Bay.[18]

ALCIDE, "Fleet forming line ahead. depth of water 20 fathoms [120 feet]."[14]

PRINCESSA, [at the rear of the British line] "...winds variable-NWtoN. weather moderate and fair, French getting under sail SWbyW 8 miles."[11]

Frenchman D'Ende, on *BORGONNE*, "...Fleet set sail, 24 sail-of-the-line, 2 frigates. Admiral signalled to form line in order of speed with Adm. Bouganville taking the lead and keeping the wind. Quite a gap between the first seven ships and the balance of the fleet. English in line to windward."[12]

DeGoussencourt, "...orders to clear decks and form in order of speed pretty well executed; but, as each ship is about 100 men short, we are forming badly." Those men were ashore transferring men and materials to smaller ships and boats to be carried up the James River to Lafayette.[11]

TORNQUIST, "...Ebb tide allowed us to set sail by cutting cables. Made hurried formation in 3/4 hour."[13]

12:30 P.M:

PRINCESSA, French fleet forming line with larboard tacks onboard. 34 sail.[18]

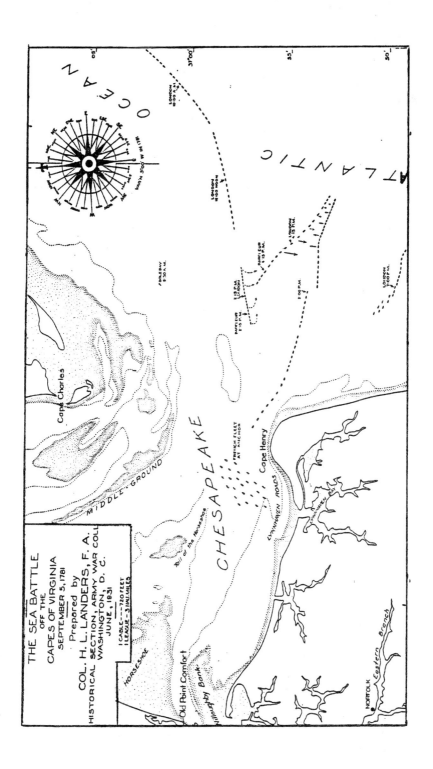

1:00 PM;

LONDON, "...course west by south, wind north-northeast, weather inclined to be squally, ...took reefs in topsails. Hauled down signal for line ahead, made signal for east-west line at one cable length. Signalled Rear Division, Adm. Drake, to make more sail.." After the battle, Adm. Graves wrote, "...as we drew near the enemy, I formed a line--first ahead, then, in such a manner as to bring my fleet parallel to the enemy."[1]

French CITOYEN, "...tide setting strong on Cape Henry, several ships are having to tack in order to clear it and get out into the ocean." [11]

Adm. Vauderuil, on LESECPTRE, wrote, "...all ships under sail, the line is forming---PLUTON, BOURGOGNE, MARSEILLAIS, DIADEME, REFLECHI, AUGUSTE, ST. ESPRIT, CATON, CEASER, etc."[11]

1:15 P.M.

LONDON, "...signalled lead ship lead more to larboard."[1]
BARFLUER, "Adm. signaled Rear..make more sail."[1]

TORNQUIST, "DeGrasse ordered Monteuil, in LANGUEDOC, to take command of the rear guard."[11]

1:30 P.M.

LONDON; "...signalled CENTAUR to keep station in the line, ...lead ship to "lead more large" [fall off the wind in order to get down closer to the French line.] A little later..."signalled RESOLUTION, AMERICA, and BEDFORD to get into their stations in the line."[1]

1:45 P.M.

BARFLUER, "signalled ALFRED make more sail."[1]

Frenchman Jenout, "CITOYEN reports clear of Cape Henry, behind VILLE DE PARIS. 17 ships clear."[11]

1:50 P.M.

BARFLUER, "...ADM. Drake made signal for INTREPID being out of station. We repeated the signal for a line ahead at 1 cable length asunder."[1]

Contemporary artist depiction of the line of battle on September 5, 1781.

Names of ships are added.

2:00 P.M.

LONDON, "...course West by South, enemy fleet... 24 ships-of-the-line, two frigates. Their Van (lead division) bearing South 3 miles, standing to East-ward with larboard (port) tacks onboard, in a line ahead."[9]

DeGoussencourt wrote, "...although free of the Cape, we are forming badly. ...only *PLUTON, BOURGOGNE, MARSEILLAIS, and DIADEME* are in the line. *REFLECHY and CATON* are next, one-half league to leeward [downwind], ... rest of fleet is a league or more to leeward of them. English are in best possible order, bearing down from the windward."[11]

2:05 P.M.

Admiral Graves, on *LONDON*, seeing that his VAN (lead ships) was getting too close to the Middle Ground shoals, ordered a preparatory signal for the fleet to "wear" [come about or turn and go on a different tack--or direction]. [9]

BARFLUER, in the VAN, "...repeated signal for fleet to wear together."[10]

PRINCESSA, in the REAR, "...repeated signal to wear and come to on the other tack."[11]

L'AINE (Fr.), "..we recognized the British fleet as the same one we fought at Martinique."[14]

2:15 P.M.

LONDON, "...made signal and 'wore' together. ...'brought to' [let the wind spill out of the sails] in order to let the center of the enemy fleet come abreast of us."[9] Admiral Graves, a traditionalist, was fighting his battle according to "the book". With this maneuver, he was trying to get the two fleets lined up abreast of each other so they could battle 'one on one' but, Adm. DeGrasse had other ideas.

SHREWSBURY, "...signal to wear. shortened sail and wore in station."[12]

BARFLUER, "...we wore on signal, as did the entire fleet. Cape Henry WbyS 2 leagues. Adm. fired a gun and put helm aweather--backed sails."[10]

After the British fleet "wore" [came about on the opposite tack], Drake's REAR division became the VAN, while Hood's VAN [lead] division became the REAR.

Frenchman Jenout, "...enemy took to port tack. Adm. signalled to head vessels to increase sail."[b]

Onboard *LESCEPTRE*, Adm. Vauderuil logged, "...Adm. de Grasse signalled his lead vessels to increase their sail." This would increase their speed and close the gap to the British. later, after the battle, he entered, "...the enemy, who were to windward, and on starboard tack, turned together and took the same tack as we, without forming their line parallel to ours. The British Rear guard [Hood's] was greatly to windward of his Van, [farther from the French] and remained their during all combat---in which it did not take part."(LeNeptune, Paris)

DEGRASSE, "fleets on same course but not parallel."[11]

2:30 P.M.
LONDON, "...Adm. signalled *BEDFORD* to get into station. signalled lead ship, *SHREWSBURY,* to lead more to starboard. (fall off the wind in order to close the gap down to the French line. JHR) also signalled fire ship, *SALAMANDER,* to prime." Sometime after the battle, Graves wrote, "...as soon as I judged our VAN able to operate, I made signal to bear away and approach." [fall off the wind and head for the enemy].

2:45 P.M.
SHREWSBURY, "...enemy in line ahead, about two cable lengths asunder [1200 ft. apart]. Center of their line west. Cape Henry West 3/4 North 2 leagues. We are to windward of the enemy about three miles."[1t]

Writing later, Adm. De Grasse noted, "...The enemy all bore away under the same sail, together before the wind. ...The fleets were on the same course, but not on parallel lines. Graves Rear Guard, under Hood, was far to windward of Drake's VAN ships"[11]

2:50 P.M.
LONDON, "signalled *ROYAL OAK* ..keep in line"[9]

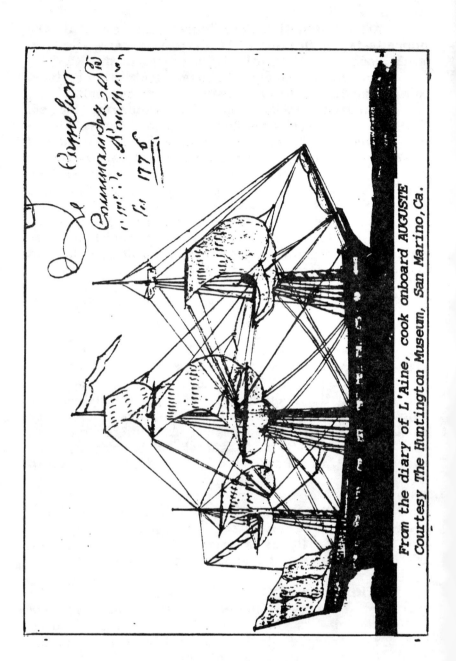

From the diary of L'Aine, cook onboard AUGUSTE
Courtesy The Huntington Museum, San Marino, Ca.

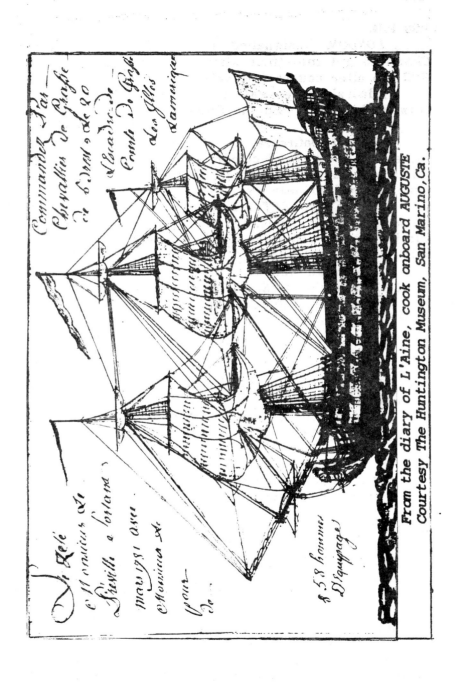

From the diary of L'Aine, cook onboard AUGUSTE
Courtesy The Huntington Museum, San Marino, Ca.

3:00 P.M.

LONDON, "...signalled ALCIDE, TERRIBLE, PRIN-CESSA to get into their stations. Signalled SHREWS-BURY to alter course to starboard." '

Admiral Graves was still trying to close the gap between his ships and the French. but,---

Admiral DeGrasse, on VILLE DE PARIS, noted, "...vessels at the head of our line, because of shifting winds and currents, were too close to the wind; they were ordered to bear away two points." [11]

French LeSCEPTRE logged, "...lead vessels, because of varying winds, are too much to windward for our line to be well formed. Adm. gave signal for lead ships to 'fall off the wind' two points." [(Le Neptune, Paris)]

Frenchman Jenout, "...LANGUEDOC takes post. AUGUSTE signals BOURGOGNE to crowd on more sail." [16]

DEnde, on BOURGOGNE, "...we are in reach of their guns, our batteries are prepared, in spite of short crews and landing parties--everyone is eager." [11]

Tornquist noted, "...French Van too much to windward. (wind is shifting around to the east). Admiral signals to run 'fuller' so the entire fleet can combine fire-power." [13]

DeGoussencourt wrote, "...the head of our line was within rifle shot of the English." [12]

French journalist, Jenout, penned, "...AUGUSTE signals BOURGOGNE to crowd on more sail." [16]

NOTE; Col. Landers' map of the Battle, page 93 shows the 3 P.M.position of the fleets.

3:10 AND 3:13 P.M.

Adm. Graves signalled his Van ships, PRINCESSA, ALCIDE, and INTREPID, under Adm. Drake, to alter course to starboard---still trying to narrow the gap between the fleets. '

3:17 P.M.

LONDON, "...repeated signal for VAN ships to keep more to starboard." [still trying to keep them closing on the French, as a result of DeGrasse's signal to his ships to fall off two points.] '

3:27 P.M.
   LONDON, "...signalled Rear ships...make more sail."[9]
   BARFLUER, "answered Adm.and repeated signal."[10]

3:30 P.M.
   BARFLUER, "...Admiral hoisted colors, so did the fleet. ... signalled to alter course more to starboard"[10]

   D'Ende, on *BOURGOGNE,* "...vessels at head of English fleet kept the wind in order to place themselves at our broadside."[11]

3:45 P.M.
   LONDON, "...course east-southeast to southeast. signalled for line-ahead at one cable-length [600 ft.]. As the enemy is advancing very slowly and evening approaches, Admiral Graves judges this is the moment for attack---makes signal for ships to BEAR DOWN AND ENGAGE THEIR OPPONENTS [blue and yellow checked flag with a white pendant above]. We filled our main top-sails and bore down." [9]
   Finally, after maneuvering for over six hours, orders to engage are flown!
   SHREWSBURY logged, "...Commander made signal for second in command (Adm. Hood, in Rear) to make more sail, although he did not do so himself."[12]

   Frenchman Jenout, "..enemy raises the signal for all vessels to follow movements of the head vessel."[30]

4:00 P.M.
   BARFLUER "...Admiral made signal with a blue and yellow checked flag, with a white pendant over it... Cape Henry west 6-9 miles."[10] (The meaning of that 'blue and yellow checked flag with a white pendant became a bone of contention over leadership and execution, between Admirals Graves and Hood, after the battle, and for years after. See Epilogue)
   PRINCESSA, "signal for line ahead...one cable length asunder. signal *TERRIBLE*... get into station."[11]

   Frenchman DeGoussencourt noted, "English *TERRIBLE* kept to windward of Drake's *PRINCESSA* which signalled 'take position in line', then fired a shot."[11]

French journalist Jenout, "...Adm. signals for all vessels to sail two quarters free."[11]

4:05 P.M.

PRINCESSA,(Drake's flagship) "...signal for each ship to bear down and attack her opponent in the enemy's line---they being in a line-ahead and standing to the southeast--their VAN about a mile to leeward."[11]

SHREWSBURY, "...Admiral made signal for the fleet to bear down and engage their opposite in the line. We were standing in with the enemy's Van. For 15 minutes we were within musket shot."[11]

4:11 P.M.

LONDON, "...hauled down signal for line-ahead so it might not interfere with signal to engage close."[1]

BARFLUER,, "Adm.fired gun to enforce last signal."

4:15 P.M.

LONDON, "...Course ESE to SE, wind NEbyN. VAN and CENTER of our fleet commence action."[1]

PRINCESSA, "...Admiral made signal to engage and soon thereafter some of the lead ships of the center division (Adm. Graves) began to engage."[11]

SHREWSBURY, "...Admiral hoisted a red flag at the fore-top-gallant mast-head to begin the action. Our Center then fired."[11]

BARFLUER, "...repeated signal to engage.[10]

(After the battle, In a letter written to Navy Secretary Stephens, Adm. Hood said, "...the signal for battle was hoisted...our Center began to engage , but at an improper distance. ...LONDON had the signal for "close action" flying as well as one for the line-ahead at half-cable. Though enemy ships were pushing on, ...our Rear division (Hood's), being barely within "random shot" distance, did not fire."[10])

D'ENDE, on BOURGOGNE [second ship in French line], "Enemy hoisted flags and firing began very strongly here and there. English TERRIBLE was at our broadside and fired ...we answere with two volleys, obliging them to move off." [11]

Tornquist noted, "...action began at musket shot distance(900ft.)....sharp fire from Bouganville's squadron, then ship to ship all through the corps."[13]

Frenchman DeGoussencourt wrote, "...British poured their first broadside into *REFLECHY*, killing Capt. deBoade, she bore away, as well as *CATO*, on which the British kept up a brisk fire."[12]

L'Aine, cook on *AUGUSTE*, wrote, "...enemy hoisted sails and began firing very strongly, here and there. English ship *TERRIBLE* was at our broadside and fired on us broadside. We answered with two consecutive volleys, obliging them to move off."[31]

4:22 P.PM.

LONDON, "...hoisted signal for line ahead again, as ships not sufficiently extended. At 4:27 she hauled down that signal and rehoisted "close action".[9]

4:30 P.M.

PRINCESSA, "...being about two cable lengths from opponent in the enemy line, we began to engage."[11]

SHREWSBURY,"...closed with our opposite number, within pistol shot---which was returned."[16]

BARFLUER, "...Van ships began to engage."[10]

WITH THE FRENCH:

LECEPTRE logged, "...enemy vessel abeam of us gave persistent fire for one/half hour, without any balls reaching us."[16] Jeptime

AUGUSTE, "...*TERRIBLE* was obliged to set sail and move off to avoid our shots. Five others came at us at the same time. Part had an intention of ramming, others of breaking the line."[31]

DeGoussencourt wrote, "...four ships in VAN cut off from the rest, constantly engaged with seven or eight enemy at close quarters. *DIADEME* constantly near Drake's *PRINCESSA*, who set fire to her with every shot. She tried to board *PRINCESSA*, which avoided her. ...turned her fire on *TERRIBLE*, which she riddled. *VILLE DE PARIS* was last to enter action."[12]

4:40 P.M.

PRINCESSA,".signalled *ALCIDE* get into station."[9]

DIADEME fires a broadside at *PRINCESSA*

PRINCESSA returns fire with a broadside

4:45 P.M.:

SHREWSBURY, "...our fore-topsail-yard came down, and soon after, our main and mizzen topsail-yards. ...still within pistol shot (150 ft)." three minutes later, "...our Captain is wounded in the thigh."[18]

PRINCESSA, "..Admiral made signal to come to closer action. SHREWSBURY's topsails are down—appearing much disabled, she quitted her station."[11]

4:55 P.M.:

SHREWSBURY,"...lower masts much damaged."[18]

PRINCESSA, "...our opponent, DIADEME, hauled up her topsails and backed her mizzen tops...we did the same in order to keep abreast of her."[11]

BARFLUER, "..Adm. made signal for ALCIDE to keep station more regular."[10]

5:00 P.M.:

LONDON, "...signaled MONTAGUE to maintain her station. VAN of enemy bore away [fell off the wind] so their center could support them."[9]

Tornquist, with the French, "..wind veered four points. Our VAN...too far to windward. DeGrasse, desiring a general engagement, signalled 'sail more freely'... to entice Graves with stern shots---he refused."[13]

DeGoussencourt diaried, "...ST. ESPIRIT first engaged Drake, but seeing DIADEME in trouble, went to her aid---opened a terrible fire which the gentlemen from Albion could not stand and hauled wind."[11]

L'Aine, on AUGUSTE, "Our head vessels slackening sail, joined the firing."[38]

Jenout, "only seven French ships not engaged. combat very violent...one no longer saw English or French through the great fire and smoke...heard men coughing...many balls fell into the water."[35]

Adm. Vauderuil, on LESCEPTRE, "...finally fired on opposite number when it was near enough for our balls to reach it. The wind having veered again, our rear guard could never rise enough to fight the enemy, who 'kept to' and concentrated their efforts on our VAN so that, although they had 20 vessels to our 24, the wind advantage gave them the means to fight

14 of our ships with 15 of theirs. This did not keep their VAN from being badly damaged."[16] [option]

DEGRASSE'S DIARY [written later], "...the wind continued to shift as much as four points, leaving our VAN too much to windward: I ordered our lead vessels to attack again. Graves VAN was roughly used."[11]

5:10P.M.
SHREWSBURY, "...Capt. Robinson lost his left leg."
5:15: "...Capt. Molloy, on *INTREPID*, hailed us and asked us to cease firing so that he might go ahead and take our place. At this time we have not a brace, bowling, or hardly a fore or main shroud left standing."[16]

Frenchman Jenout, "..part of our rear joined us and ran into those of the enemy. Our form quite close. Enemy forced sail, we did same, but darkness came."[16]

DEGOUSSENCOURT, wrote,"...*DIADEME* is unable to keep up the fight as she has only four 36 pounders and nine 18s fit for use. ...all onboard are either killed, wounded, or burned..."[11]

5:20 P.M.:
LONDON, "Adm. repeated signal for close action."[9]
BARFLUER, "...Admiral hauled down the white pennant, but kept the blue and yellow check flying under a red flag." [see Epilogue][10]

5:25 P.M.:
LONDON, "...repeated signal for close action."[9]
BARFLUER, "...Adm. hauled down the signal for line ahead, at the same time the signal for close action was flying." This log entry would indicate that Adm. Hood understood Graves signals. [see Epilogue][10]
SHREWSBURY,"..our First Lieut. was killed, we being then close alongside the enemy."[16]

5:30 P.M.
LONDON,"..course ESE. our REAR bore down."[9]
PRINCESSA, "...Van of the enemy bore up. (closed with the British)[11]
SHREWSBURY, "...we ceased firing so *INTREPID* could go ahead of us as we were not capable of

keeping the line any longer. *INTREPID* passed us to leeward, keeping her fire well up and closing with the enemy Van. Our opposite in the French line, *PLUTON*, bore out of their line with us."[t]

DEGOUSSENCOURT noted, "...contest kept up in the center for about a half hour longer. We were so tired, the Vans no longer fired."[11]

5:35 P.M.
Adm. Graves, on *LONDON*, "...signaled frigates *SOLEBAY and FORTUNEE* to come within hail..."[1] These ships were used to carry messages to other ships.

According to a letter written by Adm. Graves, after the war, as soon as Graves' signal for "line Ahead" came down, Adm. Hood signalled his Rear Division to bear down on the French Rear, but Adm. Graves countermanded that signal by rehoisting the "line ahead" and ordering *BARFLUER* back in line.

5:45 P.M.
SHREWSBURY, "..beat a retreat in order to repair rigging and 'fish' our masts. At this time we were 3 cable lengths (2000 ft.) to windward of the fleet."[t]
BARFLUER,"..enemies shots went over us."[10]

Frenchman JENOUT wrote, "...signal to head vessels to sail two quarters free. Adm. is still trying to keep the enemy's line extended."[3b]

5:50 P.M.
BARFLUER, "...we and *MONARCH* opened fire!."[10] Two hours after the signal for close action was given, Hood's Division opens fire---for the first time.

6:00 P.M.
ALCIDE, "...Van of fleet ceased firing---rear still in action. Cape Henry West, five leagues (15 miles)."[1d]
SHREWSBURY, "...all hands repairing damages."[t]
TERRIBLE,"..left off engaging, all hands employed repairing rigging. Sails much cut. Four men killed, 26 wounded. Chain and haul pumps constantly going."[1]

French journalist Jenout recorded, "...signal to hold close. Enemy has ceased firing."[3b]

6:05 P.M.
PRINCESSA, "...Admiral hauled down signal for the line. Enemy's Van bearing up, shot ahead of us; we engaged them as they passed---to their eighth ship which bore up and set her foresail."[11]

6:10 P.M.
PRINCESSA, "...ceased firing, enemy at too great a distance. Our center still in action. Enemy rear so far to leeward that few of our Rear got into action."[11]

6:15 P.M.
LONDON, "...Course ESE, wind NEbyE Admiral sent *SOLEBAY* to ships in Rear and *FORTUNEE* to those in Van with orders for ships to keep in parallel line with the enemy and well abreast during the night, so that in the morning when he signalled for close action, every ship would be as near the enemy as possible."[9]

6:23 P.M.
LONDON, "...hauled down signal for close action; signalled for line ahead, one cable length asunder."[9]
BARFLUER, "...Admiral hauled down the signal for close action and made the signal for the line ahead--- we acknowledged---hauled the wind and tacked in order to gain our station."[9] Once again, Hood's flagship acknowledged they understood the signals for close action and line ahead.

6:30 P.M.
LONDON, "...firing has ceased on both sides."[9]
SHREWSBURY, "...Admiral hauled down signal for close action. Some shots were fired from both sides."[1e]
ALCIDE, "...all of fleet has ceased firing."[1d]

JENOUT ,"...firing ceased; signal for assembly".[3b]

* * * * *

* * * * *

In approximately two hours and twenty minutes, the battle was over. Damage to ships ran from crippling, in the Vanguards of both fleets, to minor and none in the Rears of both fleets.

DAMAGE REPORTS

In the French Line:

Admiral DeGrasse recorded; three officers killed--18 wounded, 209 men killed or wounded.

DIADEME, was reported to have lost 120 men, no sails or rigging standing and taken 125 balls in her hull--12 under water; she would have been abandoned if the seas had run high.[11]

L'Aine, noted *AUGUSTE* took a number of balls in her hull, sails were riddled and rigging much cut.[11]

D'ENDE on *BOURGOGNE* recorded, "...we had a dozen men killed in this battle and many wounded. Several men were burned by fire from several cartridges which caught from the fire of the guns. We had a number of balls in the hull...our sails were riddled and a great part of the rigging cut." [11]

REFLECHY reported Capt. Deboade killed.

[Obviously, other French ships were damaged, but damage reports were not found. JHR]

In the British line:

Admiral Graves reported 12 ships lost a total of 90 men killed and 246 wounded. The seven ships of the REAR had no casualties and very little damage.[1]

SHREWSBURY, ...26 men killed, 46 wounded. fore-mast shot through in three places, fore-yard hit in three places. Four shot through mainmast, main-yard and main topmast-yard shot through. Mizzenmast almost cut through. Six studding-sail booms shot away. Hull so badly damaged that when larboard tacks were on-board she made 18 inches of water in four hours.[11]

PRINCESSA, Admiral Drake's flagship, ...main topmast shot through in three places. Main topsail-yard shot away....hole through the middle of the fore-topmast. Five yard-arms shot off. Longboat and cutter much damaged. Many sail, shrouds, and rigging cut."

AJAX, ...Much main-deck damage. Head of mainmast wounded, mizzen-topmast shot through. Main trussel-tree shivered by shot. Fore-top-gallant mast shot away. Many sails, shrouds, and rigging cut."

INTREPID, Head rails shot through. 65 holes in starboard side, nineteen between wind and water. Rudder damaged. Upper quarter-deck shot to pieces. Two holes in bowsprit, 3 in foremast, two in mainmast. Sails and rigging much damaged. All boats damaged."

TERRIBLE,...two large shot in foremast, main topsails damaged. Several shot between wind and water. Pumps blown--making two feet of water in 25 minutes.'

LONDON, Mainmast and foremast dangerously wounded; standing and running rigging much cut, sails much damaged, 3 guns dismounted, 2 men killed, 18 wounded.

* * * * *

Both fleets spent the evening of September 5th, repairing damages, tending the wounded, and trying to keep the other ships in sight. *ALCIDE* reported the French fleet about four miles away. At 9 P.M. *MONTAGUE* hailed *LONDON* to advise that she was so badly damaged she could not maintain her position in line. *FORTUNEE*, one of the messenger frigates, hailed to advise that *SHREWSBURY's* Capt. Robinson had to have his leg amputated and asked to be relieved of command, *INTREPID* was much disabled, and *PRINCESSA* expected her main-topmast to fall at any time.

CHAPTER NINE
WITH COLORS CASED:

At 2:30 A.M. on the 6th, *ALCIDE* reported her mizzen top-gallant mast carried away. At 8 A.M., the weather was calm, fleet...in line ahead, French fleet still to leeward about 3 miles. *INTREPID* and *SHREWS-BURY* asked to "speak" the Admiral; they were much disabled, carpenters were busy re-rigging new fore-yards and stopping holes in sides, sailmakers were busy repairing wounded sails and "bending" new ones.

Admiral Graves noted that the French did not appear to have been damaged as much as the English, though their VAN must have experienced a great loss.

French journalist Jenout observed that his ships masts were much damaged--but standing. The British had many vessels damaged....3 had no main-topmasts, 1 no foremast, and 1 no bowsprit. [1]

At 10 A.M., Admiral Graves dispatched *MEDEA* to reconnoiter the Chesapeake. Shortly, Capt. Colpoys went aboard *SHREWSBURY* to relieve Capt. Robinson. Adm.Drake shifted his flag from *PRINCESSA* to *ALCIDE*. *PRINCESSA* got down her main top-sail yard and main-topmast ...so shot away as to be unserviceable.

12 NOON: *PRINCESSA*, "...Cape Henry N47dW 19 leagues (57 miles), weather moderate and clear with winds at NE. *TERRIBLE* reported that she was taking on water so fast the pumps could not keep ahead. [2]

By dusk on the 7th, while repairing ship in the morning and maneuvering in the afternoon--with the French trying to gain the windward position--the two fleets had drifted so far south that *BARFLUER* logged that Roanoke Island [present day Manteo, N.C.]could be seen in the southwest about 12-15 miles.

The afternoon of the 8th was squally with rain—many ships reefed sails. Admiral de Grasse tried to work to windward; and at one point signalled his fleet to bear down on the enemy and steer within pistol shot. Admiral Graves, at first, appeared to accept the challenge, but, seeing he would be disadvantaged, tacked the British fleet away. Around 6 P.M., *MEDEA* rejoined the fleet with a report that *CHARON*, *GUADALOUPE, & FOWEY* had been stripped of armament for the defense of Yorktown.

In the upper Chesapeake, at Baltimore, American and French troops marched through town, anticipating boarding transports for the trip down the Bay.

At noon on the ninth, British *TERRIBLE* reported to Admiral Graves, "...we are in distress. our leaks since yesterday have increased alarmingly: water has gained two feet in 25 minutes---against 6 hand pumps. ....in a heavy wind we cannot save her. Pumps are in a very bad state. ..have thrown the lower deck guns over-board and, unless you forbid it, will do the same with the forecastle and quarter-deck guns."[1]

By the 10th, the fleets had lost sight of each other: De Grasse took his back to Cape Henry. Around noon, Adm. Graves called for a conference with Admirals Drake and Hood. When Hood asked where were the French, Graves said he did not know. Graves then asked for their opinion on the best course of action. Hood said, "...go to the Chesapeake to aid Lord Cornwallis, but it is probably too late." The Council of War, after receiving certification from her officers that *TERRIBLE.* was beyond saving, decided to scuttle her.

On the 11th, Graves ordered *TERRIBLE*, prepared for sinking. The day was spent removing all possible stores and men: at 7 P.M. ship's carpenters went aboard and scuttled her [knocked holes in the hull so the sea could come in.]. At 8 P.M. she was set afire in several places, shortly after midnight she blew up. The English fleet then headed for New York.

At the mouth of the Chesapeake, on the 11th, *AUGUSTE* sighted a strange sail---it turned out to be the frigate *CONCORDE* which signaled that Adm. de Barras squadron was at anchor inside the Capes. De Barras brought with him *DUC de BOURGOGNE--80 guns, NEPTUNE--80 guns, CONQUERANT--74, PROVENCE--74, EVEILLE--64, JASON--64, ARDENT--64, ROMULUS--54, and CONCORDE--40*: the French armada now numbered 31 ships-of-the-line and several frigates---the Chesapeake was blocked. The English at Yorktown were trapped. Admiral de Grasse could now turn his attention to bringing the American and French troops down from the upper Bay and completing the unloading of the siege cannon and the troops of St. Simon, for transporting to Jamestown.

Generals Washington and Rochambeau, with their staffs, arrived in Williamsburg on September 14th. Washington wrote de Grasse--"...I take particular pleasure in congratulating your Excellency on the glory of having driven the British fleet from the coast and taken two of their frigates. These happy events, and the decided superiority of your fleet, give us the happiest presages of a most complete success in our combined operations in the Bay. ..."[16]

Three days later, Washington, Rochambeau, Chastellux, Duportail, Knox, and Col. Alexander Hamilton boarded Admiral de Grasse's flagship, *VILLE DE PARIS*, anchored in Lynnhaven Bay, for a conference to plan the strategy for the siege of Yorktown. According to Parke Custis, Washington's nephew, Adm. de Grasse greeted Washington with the typical French greeting of a kiss on both cheeks, and called him "mon cher petite general"; as Washington was over six foot two, this caused Gen. Henry Knox to break out in laughter. There was much discussion about the length of de Grasse's stay: although his instructions stated he should depart by October 15th, de Grasse took it upon himself to commit to stay until November 1st.

In New York, on September 24th, British Commander in Chief, General Sir Henry Clinton called a council of war to plan a course of action in regard to

General Lord Cornwallis' situation at Yorktown. It was decided that 5000 troops would be embarked on the ships of the fleet, and a joint army-navy operation be undertaken to relieve him. With the addition of Admiral Digby's squadron, which had just arrived from England, the British fleet would now number 23 ships-of-the-line. They were to set sail as soon as repairs could be made—hopefully by October 5th. A courier ship was dispatched to advise Cornwallis of this. But, Sir Henry had failed to grasp the tenor of his situation—repairs were not the only problem—there was dissension within his command.

In a diary entry made in early October, Lt. Frederick Mckenzie, an observant junior officer on Clinton's staff, noted, "...If the Navy are not a little more active, they will not get a sight of the Capes of Virginia before the end of the month, and then will be too late. They do not seem to be hearty in the business, or to think that saving that army is an object of such material consequence. One of the Captains said that the loss of two line-of-battle ships...in effecting the relief, is of more consequence than losing the army. Sir Samuel Hood seems to be the only man of that Corps who is urgent about the matter. ..."[15] On the same day, Lt. John Peebles, another aide, noted in his diary, "...the Navy people do not seem to be in a hurry on this occasion."[16]

On Sept. 25th, Admiral de Grasse, in Lynnhaven Bay, heard of the arrival of Adm. Digby's fleet at New York. Apprehensive about being caught at anchor in the Bay, he proposed he take his fleet and cruise outside the Capes. After being prevailed upon by Gen. Washington's personal envoy, Gen. Lafayette, de Grasse advised that he would reposition his ships, anchoring them at the mouth of the Chesapeake in such a way that they could fight at anchor or under sail without "disposting" themselves from the Bay. That same day the balance of the French transports arrived from Baltimore with the remainder of the American and French troops; debarked at College Creek, near Jamestown, they were marched to the siege lines at York.

By the 28th of September, all of the troops, siege guns, and munitions were in place surrounding Yorktown, and the "investiture" began: Much has already been written about that battle and further detail is not needed here. A fitting finish can be put to the story with a letter written by General Henry Knox to his much loved wife Lucy, who was staying with Mrs. Washington at Mount Vernon:

Camp before Yorktown,
8 AM, Friday,
October 19, 1781

I have detained William until this last moment so I might be the first to communicate the good news to the charmer of my soul! A glorious moment for America! This day Cornwallis and his army march out and pile their arms before our victorious army.

They will have the same honors as our garrison at Charleston, that is, they will not be permitted to unfurl their colours or play Yankee Doodle.

I shall see you, if possible, on the 12th of next month. How much I long for that happy moment.

HENRY KNOX[4]

* * * * *

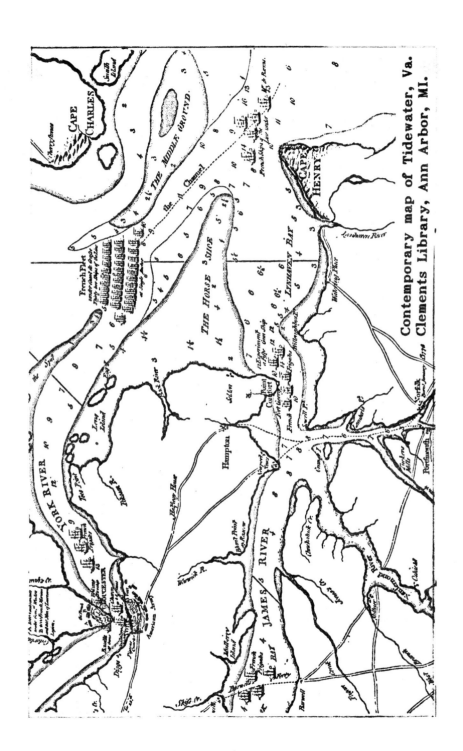

Contemporary map of Tidewater, Va. Clements Library, Ann Arbor, MI.

On October 20th General Washington went back to Lynnhaven Bay to confer with Admiral DeGrasse. He urged the Admiral to transport a force, commanded by Major General Lafayette, to the Cape Fear River[Wilmington,N.C.] so they could take that post. De Grasse agreed.

On the 24th, an express rider came in from New Jersey bringing dispatches from General David Foreman telling of a British fleet leaving New York harbor, 26 sail-of-the-line, frigates, transports, and fireships.

On the 28th, Admiral DeGrasse sent word to Washington that a British fleet of 36 sail had been sighted off the Capes: after maneuvering around for two days, they set sail. The belated attempt of General Clinton and Admiral Graves to rescue General Cornwallis set sail for New York: They had decided not to attempt to breach the Blockade of the Chesapeake.

DeGrasse also advised that, because of time constraints, he was withdrawing his offer to transport troops to Wilmington.

* * * * *

Shortly before he took his fleet out of the Capes and back to the West Indies, Admiral DeGrasse wrote Washington, "...Allow me to request you to reserve me a place in your memory. I consider myself infinitely happy to have been of some service to the United States; but, I should regard it as an advantage at least as precious, if I could flatter myself that I carried away with me your esteem and your friendship."[16]

General George Washington summed up his feelings in a letter he wrote to Congress, "...I wish I had it in my power to express to Congress, how much I feel myself indebted to the Count de Grasse and the fleet under his command."[1]

EPILOGUE:

Over the years much has been written about the confusion of signals within the British fleet on the day of the Battle Off The Capes. Admiral Hood wrote a long letter to his friend George Jackson, Assistant Secretary of the Admiralty, complaining of Admiral Graves leadership during the battle. He complained of missed opportunities and confusing signals. This writer is of the opinion that Admiral Hood did not go out of his way to help "seize the glorious opportunity" of which he spoke. It could be said that he held back out of petulance---except for Graves one year of seniority, Hood would have commanded the British fleet.

Hood made much of the fact that Graves flew the signal for the "line ahead" and that for "close action" simultaneously; yet, as early as 1756, Admiral Hawke in his "memo of instructions" said, "...when sailing in the line of battle...and I would have the ship that leads...to lead down to the enemy, I will hoist a Dutch Jack under my flag...then every ship in the squadron is to steer for the ship of the enemy that...it must be her lot to engage...notwithstanding I shall keep the signal for the line ahead flying..." [emphasis added]

In his book, "Signals and Instructions(1776-1794)", J.S. Corbett says Admiral Arbuthnot, of the North American Command, instructed in 1779, "...if at any time, while engaged with the enemy, I shall judge it necessary to come to a closer engagement, I will hoist a flag, checquered blue and yellow, under the signal for engagement (red)...then every ship is to engage the enemy as close as possible." [emphasis added]. In 1781, he added, "...when I would have each ship steer for and engage his opponent in the enemy's line, I will hoist the signal for close action and a white pennant over it...". THIS IS THE SIGNAL THAT HOOD'S OWN SHIP, BARFLUER, LOGGED AT 4:00 PM.

Some writers say the confusion came from Adm. Graves use of Adm. Arbuthnot's signals while Hood, coming from the West Indies fleet was accustomed to Admiral Rodney's signals: Hood had been second in command to Rodney for about 15 months. Again from Corbett, "...if at any time while engaged with the enemy, the Commander in Chief [Admiral Rodney] judges it necessary to come to a closer engagement, he will hoist a flag—half blue-half white, under the signal for engaging...whereupon every ship is to engage the enemy as close as possible." [emphasis added]. Was there confusion as to the difference in flags---blue and yellow checked, and half blue/half white? Admiral Rodney, in April of 1780, three months after Admiral Hood arrived in the West Indies, instructed, "...should the ships of the squadron, at any time, not clearly discern or understand the meaning of any signal made from the ship my flag is in, they are to make known the same to me by hoisting the Dutch Jack at the main top-gallant mast..." The log of Hood's own flagship, *BARFLUER* shows no request for a clarification of any signal.

Perhaps the most clinching rebuttal is found in the actions of Admiral Drake and his division. Drake's division had been serving with Admiral Rodney in the West Indies, along with Hood's division. They came North with Hood. Drake never gave any indication of not understanding Graves' signals. As *PRINCESSA* (Drakes flagship), *SHREWSBURY, and ALCIDE* were in the thick of the battle and received the heaviest damages, it is obvious they came to a close action.

ON THE FRENCH SIDE;
Some writers have said that Admiral de Grasse, although far superior to Graves, failed to win a "decisive" victory: de Grasse fought his battle his way! As John Paul Jones wrote in 1791, "...in general, I may say that it has been the policy of French Admirals in the past, to neutralize the power of their adversaries, if possible, by grand maneuvers rather than destroy it by grand attack...the French tactical system partakes of the chivalry of the French people;

on the wave, as on the field of honor, they wish to wound rather than kill the enemy."

Some writers [this one included] have speculated as to the outcome of the Battle Off The Capes, if Admiral Rodney, instead of returning to England, had brought his fleet to North America. He would have commanded the British fleet at the Battle instead of Admiral Graves. Even Admiral Hood said, sometime after the battle, that if Rodney had led the West Indies squadron up, he would have been in charge at the Chesapeake; and, the 5th of September would have been a glorious day for Great Britain.

Regardless of all the varying opinions, nothing should be allowed to detract from the importance of the contribution of Admiral de Grasse, and his fleet, to the conquest of Cornwallis. With reenforcement or rescue blocked at the Capes, his army backed up to the cliffs of the York, and encircled on the landside by the combined forces of Washington and Rochambeau, it was only a matter of time and attrition before Cornwallis had to choose between annihilation or surrender---On October 19th, he chose surrender!

Except for scattered skirmishes in the south, and formalities of peace negotiations, that day, October 19, 1781, marked the successful termination of our War For Independence.

WATCH FOR

'BURN BRIGHT THE FLAME'

The story of "landside" events in Tidewater, Virginia during the American Revolution.

The Battle of Great Bridge-1775

The burning of Norfolk-1776

The questionable actions of Gen. Charles Lee.

Collier's raid on Hampton Roads-1779

Benedict Arnold's rampage up the James River in 1780, and the occupation of Portsmouth.

Our North Carolina Friends.

Gen. William Phillips campaign in Virginia-1781.

Gen. Earl Charles Cornwallis march through Virginia, and occupation of Portsmouth.

Major General Lafayette and General Steuben in Virginia.-1781

The siege and Surrender at Yorktown-1781

by J.H. ROBERTSON

Anticipated publication late 1998.